SOMEWHERE
IN THE
WESTERN PACIFIC

Marie Sturdevant's "Somewhere in the Western Pacific" brings a different view to the stories portrayed through war letters of our WWII Veterans. Marie's story of discovery comes from the letters of her father, Sgt. Sven Sandstrom, an armorer with the 342nd Fighter Squadron. Sgt. Sandstrom is one of the hundreds-of-thousands of support guys making sure the beans and bullets get to the tip of the spear. For every combat troop there were 10-20 support personnel taking care of the combat troops; these were the unsung mechanics, cooks, mail carriers and truck drivers, all supplying the ammunition, bombs, spare parts, fuel, food, medical attention, transportation, and so much more to secure victory in the Pacific. Even though these guys never pulled a trigger in anger, they still experienced the same hardships of the Pacific theater, the endless heat, rain, mud and rotten living conditions, and being separated from their families and friends. Sgt. Sandstrom reveals through his letters to "Ginny" his beloved future wife, his experiences in the Pacific and how he and thousands of other guys tried to maintain some kind of normalcy with a connection to home through letters to loved ones.

The letters of Sgt. Sandstrom bring a very personal and human element to the daily, non-stop grind of wartime ground operations, and that these men were determined to succeed regardless of the cost. It shows that life as they knew it didn't stop because of the war, but rather life went on in spite of the war.

It's through the faded memories and personal accounts of our Veterans through letters such as these that our future generations will come to understand the character and fabric of those who fought and served in WWII. They will learn that these men were not born fighters – rather they were young, scared, and in the end, simply doing their jobs in incredibly tough and challenging environments. And they will learn that these guys, by just doing their job, proved the defining characteristic of their greatness.

James Bina

President, 345th Bomb Group Association
Second Generation

SOMEWHERE
IN THE
WESTERN PACIFIC

The War Through
The Eyes Of My Father

Marie L. Sturdevant

ISBN-13: 978-0615843193
ISBN-10: 0615843190

Wartime letters, written over a half century ago, between soldier and sweetheart, family and friends, provide perspectives of the times as unique as the individuals who wrote them. In today's world, where communication is almost instantaneous, we can only begin to imagine what it may have been like to wait days, weeks and sometimes months before receiving news from home and abroad concerning the safety and well-being of loved ones.

The stories that unfold in the following pages come from the letters my dad wrote to his sweetheart, who became his wife two years after returning home from overseas. These letters provide a rare glimpse into the lives and long-distance relationship of my father and mother over a decade before I was born.

While serving overseas during World War II, censorship regulations prohibited soldiers from identifying their exact location. As for my father, his letters indicated he was stationed "Somewhere in the Western Pacific." A careful study of history, along with his letters, have enabled me to piece together more specifics of where he was and what life was like for him as an armorer of P-47 Thunderbolts, and P-51 Mustangs, assigned to the 342nd Fighter Squadron of the 348th Fighter Group in the Pacific Theater.

It is with love and admiration
that I dedicate this book to my parents:

Sven Louis "Louie" Sandstrom
and
Hildur Virginia "Ginny" Carlstrom Sandstrom

342nd Fighter Squadron insignia

CONTENTS

Acknowledgements

Completing *Somewhere in the Western Pacific* was the result of almost two years of reading, researching and writing There were several people who helped me through the many phases of bringing this project to completion; editing, formatting, sharing the stories of life during WWII, and giving me encouragement along the way:

To my husband and best friend, **Preston**: thank you for your encouragement and support. It was your belief in my abilities that gave me the confidence needed to bring my dream of writing this book to a reality. Your expertise with computers helped with the technical aspects of creating the finished manuscript. I also appreciated sharing with you those moments of discovery as I read through the letters and pieced together some of the intimate details of this story.

To **René Palmer Armstrong**, author of *Wings and a Ring: Letters of War and Love from a WWII Pilot:* thank you for being my mentor and very special friend throughout the process of writing this book. I have learned so much from you as you guided me through the many steps of bringing this book to completion. I enjoyed the times we talked and shared our individual stories and connections with the Greatest Generation. You have inspired me in so many ways and I am forever grateful for everything you have done.

To **Bill Simon** and **Jim Bina**: thank you for reading my manuscript and sharing your thoughts and suggestions. It is a very special privilege and honor to have received your endorsements.

This book includes several WWII vintage photos from my father's personal collection. To my cousin, **Birgitta Blomqvist**, thank you for helping me with picture formatting. I greatly appreciated the time you spent with me, teaching me the finer points of resizing and bringing out more detail in my father's photographs using computer technology.

To **Preston and Audrey Sturdevant** (Dad and Mom Sturdevant): thank you for sharing your stories of life on the home front. I enjoyed listening to your stories and those from many others of the Greatest Generation. I consider it a privilege to have had the opportunity to hear these firsthand accounts of life during World War II. Dad Sturdevant, a former Navy corpsman and World War II veteran, read a couple of chapters of my work and made some edits and suggestions which enhanced my presentation. My regret is that he passed away before I was able to complete this book, but I am grateful to have received his approval and the thumbs up on the few chapters I was able to share with him.

To **Lawrence Hickey and The International Historical Research Associates**: thank you for your permission to use the picture of Bob Hope and Frances Langford when sharing the story of the USO camp show in Wakde, New Guinea in August of 1944

I was missing some information about my dad's squadron from their beginning through shipping out to their first overseas operational base in Port Moresby, New Guinea. To **John Stanaway**, author of *Kearby's Thunderbolts: The 348th Fighter Group in World War II*, and **Schiffer Publishing Ltd.**, thank you for granting me permission to use information from your book, making it possible to add more detail to the early days of the 348th Fighter Group.

To my children, **Christine** and **Robert**, this book is for you. It is because of you that I wanted to share this story. You have given me the motivation to complete this work as I wanted to be able to connect you with the grandfather whom you never had the chance to know.

To **my parents** and to **the Greatest Generation**: I thank you for the sacrifices you made that we may enjoy our freedoms and a better way of life.

Finally, and most of all, I give thanks to **God.** It is through His Grace that my life is rich in many blessings; my life, my faith and the love of my family and friends. To Him, all glory and honor.

Foreword

In today's world of electronic communication, the power found in the written word has almost become a lost art. First-hand accounts of the stories of wartime through the words written on paper seven decades ago compel us to dig deeper into what made these groups of people, collectively known as the Greatest Generation, be so amazing.

Letters became the very lifeline between a soldier and his family and friends. For the soldier away from home, reading through letters sharing even the everyday, and sometimes mundane happenings of life were enough to make him homesick. Because of censorship, soldiers were not able to share their locations and battle details. Trying to convey their fears and hardships while not compromising their nation's security was a real challenge.

As a child of a WWII veteran and an author of a book about a WWII B-25 pilot, I am ever so aware of the fact that we are daily losing their personal histories. Letters of soldiers to their family members and friends provide us with a rare glimpse into the very heart and emotions of these individuals.

Family members and historians are actively working to capture these stories while our WWII veterans are still with us. Unfortunately, as in my case and as with countless other children of these veterans, their personal stories will be lost forever because the veterans never shared their stories.

Sometimes the treasures of their personal experiences are found in unlikely places like junk stores and estate sales. More often than not, these jewels are overlooked and discarded as mere papers from some long-forgotten person. At other times, the papers fall into the hands of individuals who truly understand their worth. I had the privilege of bringing a B-25 pilot's story to life after my husband found 295 letters in a junk store. I was entrusted with his letters, diligently worked to find the soldier's family, did the historical research to determine what part he played in the war effort, and spent a total of four and one-half years to bring his story to fruition.

It was because of my book, *Wings and a Ring*, that I had the privilege of meeting Marie L. Sturdevant. Her discovery of her father's letters brought a whole new understanding of who her parents were and what sacrifices they each had to make during WWII. Although her father, Sven Louis "Louie" Sandstrom, never spoke of his experiences to Marie, she was able to research his activities through his letters and the activities of her father's unit, piecing together this amazing glimpse into the lives of her parents long before she was born. What a remarkable gift given to a child.

Complete with his sharing of stories about red alerts and diving into fox-holes, of listening to the top musical hits of the day like *Pistol Packin' Mama*, and of describing what he saw while meeting up with the natives in New Guinea, the reader will have a better understanding of what Louie Sandstrom experienced as an armorer of the P-47 Thunderbolts and P-51 Mustangs while overseas from June of 1943 through November of 1945.

While reviewing *Somewhere in the Western Pacific*, I found myself recalling similar situations experienced by the veteran whom I wrote about in the 345th Bomb Group. The further I read, it became apparent that Louie Sandstrom's unit, the 342nd Fighter Squadron of the 348th Fighter Group, was stationed in many of the of the same locations found in my book. The timeline provided in Marie's book provides a great overview of the worldwide events during WWII.

Because of Marie's efforts, she will leave a legacy for her family members for generations to come. This work, plus many others like hers, will ensure that the collective memories of the Greatest Generation will always be remembered.

René Palmer Armstrong

Author, *Wings and a Ring*

Member, 345th Bombardment Group Association

Ordinary People,
Extraordinary Times

Wars are fought by heroes, but not of their own making. Ordinary people do not enter a conflict with the intention of becoming a hero, nor do they consider themselves one after the fact. Circumstances happen, and then out of instinct or character, split second decisions are made, sometimes proving to be heroic in nature.

There is little doubt in my mind that World War II was fought, not by the heroes as we see in war movies, but rather by ordinary people who were living in extraordinary times. As I have read through stories and listened to those who lived through it, I am amazed by the courage, strength and fortitude of these individuals. Many came from simple backgrounds, and learned their values and life lessons as they grew up against the backdrop of the Great Depression. Perhaps this was the greatest builder of character that set the stage to make the sacrifices for the war effort. The drive to fight enemies on foreign soils that threatened that which was most near and dear, "faith, family, comrades and country," and make sacrifices on the home front, were characteristics of the people living in these times. This is what made these ordinary people into real heroes.

Each generation is the product of the previous generations, shaped by the circumstances of the times in which they live. We learn by the examples set by the previous generation, but we are shaped by world events, prosperity or poverty, and the general philosophies of the leaders of the day.

Generations come and go, leaving their unique marks on the pages of history. As the sun sets on the Greatest Generation, time grows short in gathering their personal stories. These individuals, who were born between the early 1900's and the mid 1920's, came of age in the years of the Great Depression, and then went on to fight in World War II, making the common sacrifices both on the battlefront and home front. Numerous stories have been lost because many veterans didn't share what they had experienced while serving in the war. Those fortunate enough to have letters that were written during these times of war and sacrifice, have access to firsthand accounts and unique perspectives of the events and emotions of the day.

Both of my parents were born in 1921 in Worcester, Massachusetts, and grew up in a section of Worcester called Quinsigamond Village. This small community was mostly settled by Swedish immigrants who came to America in the mid to late 1800's and early 1900's. They were hard-working, conservative people. Everyone in the neighborhood knew each other as they cultivated strong bonds through church and in those casual encounters with one another in one of the many shops and stores throughout the village. Most of the women in this community were skilled homemakers, having learned their art of cooking and handiwork in the old country. Many of the men in the village were employed by the American Steel and Wire, Co., the mill around which Quinsigamond Village was built. Others found their trade or employment in one of the local shops or businesses. As the children of these Swedish immigrants became young adults, some followed in the footsteps of their parents in profession and trade, while others, including my mother and father, sought opportunities outside of the village. Norton Company, one of the largest employers of the Swedes in Worcester County was across the city, in an area of Worcester called Greendale. Norton's, founded in 1885, was one of the world's leading manufacturers of abrasives. This is where both of my parents were employed in the days leading up to the war.

My parents and their contemporaries enjoyed the simple pleasures of life as they grew up in the time of the Great Depression. There were band concerts at Greenwood Park and dances at the S.A.C. (Scandinavian Athletic Club) where they bonded with friends whom they called the old gang. Sometimes they would meet at the local soda fountain, where a nickel could buy you an ice cream treat. This group of friends also shared in social time at the Nordic Lodge, a local chapter of the Vasa Order of America, where they could enjoy their commonalities in their Swedish heritage and traditions. They didn't have much by way of money and possessions, and yet they had abundant lives, in a time they often referred to as the good old days. They found joy in gathering with family and friends, and a feeling of being safe within this quaint and peaceful community, where decency, courtesy, and honesty were among the common virtues of the day.

(From the Sven L. Sandstrom collection)
My dad, Sven L. Sandstrom, graduated from South High School
in Worcester, Massachusetts in 1939.

After the United States entered the war in 1941, one by one the young men enlisted or were drafted into military service. Some headed for the war in Europe, while others were sent to the war in the Pacific. And they left their boyhood innocence behind.

My parents met through their group of friends and had their first date at a Halloween party in October of 1941. They married on November 29, 1947, two years after my dad returned home from the war. Much of their time getting to know each other is contained in the letters that were written to each other during the war years. While I only have the letters my dad wrote to my mom, his letters answered many of the questions and responded to many of the concerns my mom had written to him. Both experienced the war, but from different perspectives - the battlefront and the home front. Both were involved in the war effort in making the common sacrifices of the times.

My dad never spoke with me about his experiences in the war. He, like many others who returned from overseas, didn't talk about the things that were seen, and instead buried the images of war beneath the levels of consciousness. My dad had a strong sense of pride in the squadron with which he served, as evident in the letters he wrote. He had a deep patriotic spirit, that remained in him all through his life as he connected with other members of the Chester P. Tuttle American Legion Post 279. But he never spoke with me about the war. That part of his life remained a mystery. I lost that opportunity in knowing an essential part of who he was when he passed away on December 15, 1987.

Much of my perception of what life was like during the Depression and the war came through the stories my mom and other family members and friends shared with me. After my mom passed away on February 9, 2007, I found a box containing letters and pictures she had saved. I began looking through them and found the letters and pictures my dad sent to my mom during the war - a hidden treasure and perspective on the war years as seen through the eyes of my father. He was an ordinary man called to duty to serve in the most violent war in history. His words, documented in these letters, are used in this book to describe what his experiences were like. Although he makes some references to the war and the successes of his squadron, as allowed by censorship rules, he wrote a lot about what life was like in the military, on the bases and overseas in the jungles of the Western Pacific Islands. He wrote about the things that were important to him, and often expressed a longing to return home. I have presented his words as he wrote them, and made no edits. He expressed his thoughts using the language of the day, including slang which would be considered derisive by today's standards. He, like other Americans, used terms like Japs and Nips when referring to the Japanese people. Some of their opinions and hence their language resulted from the images they had seen in the pre-war newsreels which depicted the Japanese as ruthless warriors, who murdered and brutalized civilians living in China and Southeast Asia. Sometimes my father wrote with humor, which was a coping mechanism in dealing with the stresses of being near the front lines of the war.

I have also gathered stories of what life was like on the home front, and they are included in the chapter, *Total War, Total Effort: The Home Front*. Without the sacrifices, efforts and contributions of those on the home front, it is uncertain what the outcome of the war would have been. It was the total effort involving every man, woman and child that saved the free world from tyranny, the oppressive rule of the Axis Alliance of Germany, Italy and Japan. The stories of life on the home front come from recollections of stories shared by my mom, and stories told by my father-in-law, Dr. Preston J. Sturdevant, Jr., and my mother-in-law, Audrey K. Sturdevant. Other family members and friends also shared their memories of life during the late 1930's and 1940's.

My father-in-law grew up in Forty Fort, Pennsylvania, and my mother-in-law grew up in Wilkes Barre, Pennsylvania. Both were in their teens at the time of the war, and remembered the hardships of those days. They shared stories of what it was like to do with less because of rationing of many everyday essentials, including gasoline and some food items. They both told stories of scrap drives, blackouts and air raids. My father-in-law was an air raid messenger, and remembered well what it was like to deliver messages in the darkness of the night during the air raid drills. These stories help to complete the overall sense of what it was like living in the dark days when the world was at war.

Most of the images in this book are from my dad's collection of photographs taken during his time of service from 1942-1945. The images of letters, V-Mail, war ration books, and gasoline ration stickers are from my collection, and the collection passed down from my mother. Other images have been cited and given appropriate credit with the caption. The stories of life in the military that unfold in the following pages come from excerpts of the letters my dad wrote to his sweetheart, my mom, while serving in the Army Air Corps during the war. They are dated from June 1942 through November 1945, covering his basic training through deployment in the Western Pacific theater of operations. They are the stories and experiences of ordinary people caught up in the most catastrophic war in history.

Chapter

2

Total War, Total Effort: The Home Front

World War II, more than any other war, had significant home front support that involved citizens of all ages and all walks of life. It was the combined effort of those on the battle front and the home front that helped secure the freedoms that were threatened by the powers of the Axis Alliance of Germany, Italy and Japan.

As people throughout the world were trying to recover from the devastating effects of the massive economic downturn of the 1930's, known as the Great Depression, the clouds of war were gathering over Southeast Asia, Africa, and Europe. Among the root causes of war was the failure of the Treaty of Versailles. This treaty, signed at the end of World War I, treated Germany harshly and put severe restrictions on the size of their military. It forced Germany to lose some of its territory in Europe as well as give up their overseas colonies. Germany was ordered to pay reparations in gold marks, an amount equal to $33 billion. For this reason, Germany was hit particularly hard by the worldwide depression. Failure to uphold the provisions of the treaty by the great powers of Great Britain and France lead to the start of the war as Germany began rebuilding its military with threats of expansion in Europe. In addition, the newly organized League of Nations, whose purpose was to maintain world peace was ineffective in the face of the growing threat of war. The League had no military might and therefore had no power over an aggressive act by any nation other than verbal warnings and economic sanctions. The desire to maintain an isolationist policy throughout the world by the United States weakened the prestige of the League of Nations when they refused to join, even though it was U.S. President Woodrow Wilson who supported the idea of this international organization.

In September of 1931 Japan invaded Manchuria. In a General Assembly of the League of Nations, a motion was made to condemn Japan as an aggressor. The Japanese delegation walked out and gave notice of their withdrawal from the League of Nations on March 27, 1933. During the summer of 1937, the Japanese launched a full-scale invasion of China and met heavy resistance from the Chinese in Shanghai. This battle lasted longer than the Japanese had anticipated and they emerged from battle with revenge on their minds. The worst atrocity of the war happened in December of 1937 when the Japanese Imperial Army entered the capital of China and proceeded to murder Chinese civilians and soldiers. After only a few days of battle, the Japanese defeated the Chinese and were given orders to kill all captives. The brutal and torturous murder of these 300,000 Chinese, which included men, women and children, came to be known as the Rape of Nanking. This six weeks of carnage, left thousands of bodies on the streets of the Chinese capital.

Meanwhile in Europe, Nazi leader Adolph Hitler was rising to power. During this time, Hitler expressed anti-Semitic views and in the spring of 1933, Jewish owned shops were boycotted. Those who opposed the Nazi regime were arrested and sent to camps, where they were held as political prisoners. This included some Jewish people, but large scale Jewish internment didn't occur until October of 1941, when they were sent to concentration camps or later known as Nazi death camps. On November 9, 1938, a systematic attack on Jewish owned shops, homes and synagogues was carried out by a paramilitary wing of the Nazi party called the Sturmabteilung or SA. This disgraceful act was called Crystal Night or Kristallnacht, (also known as Night of Broken Glass, or Reichskristallnacht.) Jewish-owned buildings were demolished, ransacked and burned while some

Jewish people were killed or sent to concentration camps. After the German invasion of Poland in September of 1939, Britain and France declared war on Germany. The Germans continued their conquest throughout Europe until their advancement was stalled in late 1942 and early 1943.

War in Africa began when Italy, under the rule of Fascist leader Benito Mussolini, attacked Ethiopia in 1936. In November of 1936, Germany and Japan signed the Anti-Comintern Pact (directed against the Communistic International). Italy joined the pact later in 1937. On September 27, 1940, Germany, Italy and Japan signed the Tripartite Pact. This extended the terms of their alliance to include mutual assistance against any nation showing aggression towards any of its signatories. The Tripartite Pact came as a warning to the United States to remain neutral in the war, or they would be drawn into battle on two fronts. The signing of this pact or treaty formed the group known as the Axis Alliance.

Continued aggression in China, alliance with Hitler and Mussolini, and the growing threat of Japanese expansion throughout Southeast Asia, prompted the United States to sanction Japan by imposing an embargo on oil exports. Japan relied heavily on U.S. oil and steel. The United States appealed to the Japanese government for peace, but Japan continued its efforts towards expansion in Southeast Asia. If the U.S. wouldn't lift the sanction, Japan was ready to go to war.

Early afternoon, on Sunday, December 7, 1941, Japanese representatives to the Ambassador were to deliver notice to Secretary of State Cordell Hull in Washington D.C., breaking off diplomatic relations with the U.S. Then, shortly before 8:00 AM in Hawaii, just before the notice was delivered, the Japanese launched a preemptive strike against U.S. military bases, beginning with Battleship Row at Pearl Harbor, Ford Island and Hickam Airfield. U.S. decoding services had intercepted a message saying that an attack was imminent, but the warning to military officials in Hawaii came too late as the Japanese achieved total surprise. By the time the attack was finished, over 2,300 servicemen were killed along with almost 1,200 wounded. Following this attack by the Japanese Imperial Navy against U.S. military and naval bases, a declaration of war was announced by U.S. President Franklin D. Roosevelt. This came in his famous *Day of Infamy* speech made on December 8, 1941, "...I ask that the Congress declare that since the unprovoked and dastardly attack by Japan on Sunday, December 7th, 1941, a state of war has existed between the United States and the Japanese Empire." Three days later, on December 11, 1941, under the terms of the Tripartite Pact, Germany and Italy declared war on the United States, thus drawing the U.S. into global war.

It is generally agreed upon that the Great Depression ended after the United States entry into the war. The economy immediately shifted to war production, creating more jobs in manufacturing of supplies needed for the troops and the war effort. As the men were being conscripted for war, the women were taking their places in the manufacturing jobs. *Rosie the Riveter* became a cultural icon of the times, representing the role of women working on the production lines in factories manufacturing war supplies and ammunition. Veterans would often say that the men won the battles, but the women won the war.

Changes took place in the daily lives of all Americans. In his address to the nation on April 28, 1942, President Roosevelt stated, "...But there is one front and one battle where everyone in the United States -- every man, woman, and child -- is in action, and will be privileged to remain in action throughout this war. That front is right here at home, in our daily lives, and in our daily tasks. Here at home everyone will have the privilege of making whatever self-denial is necessary, not only to supply our fighting men, but to keep the economic structure of our country fortified and secure during the war and after the war. This will require, of course, the abandonment not only of luxuries but of many other creature comforts."

In general, most people willingly took up their new roles on the home front, and considered it their contribution to the war effort. Some sacrifices, though, were imposed on the American citizens by the government. In May of 1942, the United States Office of Price Administration (OPA) froze prices on many commodities. Rationing began in early 1942 and continued until the end of the war in 1945. Sugar and coffee were the first food items to be rationed. Other foods that were rationed were meats, butter and fats, cheese, canned fish, and processed food items. Rationing was a way of being sure that everyone got their fair share.

War ration books, which contained ration stamps, were issued to each American family. Rationing set limits on how much you were allowed to buy and was not based on how much money you had to spend. According to the instructions on the back of War Ration Book 3, issued in 1943, "Each stamp authorizes you to purchase rationed goods in the quantities and at the times designated by the Office of Price Administration. Without the stamps you will be unable to purchase those goods. Detailed instructions concerning the use of the book and the stamps will be issued." There were different stamps in the book which were validated on specified dates as instructed by the Local War Price and Rationing Board. The consumer was cautioned under the instructions on the back side of Book 3, "Rationing is a vital part of your country's war effort. Any attempt to violate the rules is an effort to deny someone his share and will create hardship and help the enemy...Price ceilings have also been established for your protection. Dealers must post these prices conspicuously. Don't pay more. Be guided by the rule: If you don't need it, DON'T BUY IT."

War Ration Book One, which was issued in 1942, contained sugar stamps and coffee stamps. It also contained stamps which allowed for the purchase of shoes, having one stamp valid in February 1943 through mid June for one pair and another stamp valid in June of 1943 through the end of October 1944 for a second pair. War Ration books two, three and four were issued on later dates and had different types of stamps used for different food groups. Red stamps were for meats, butter, fats, cheese and canned fish. Blue stamps were for canned, dried and frozen fruits and vegetables. There were other stamps identified with either a color or picture (for example, stamps with pictures of airplanes, tanks, aircraft carriers and artillery), which were validated on different dates for different items. Some stamps were never validated. Each consumer was issued a certain number of stamps or points which were needed to purchase items within certain major groups. The point system allowed for some consumer preference and flexibility.

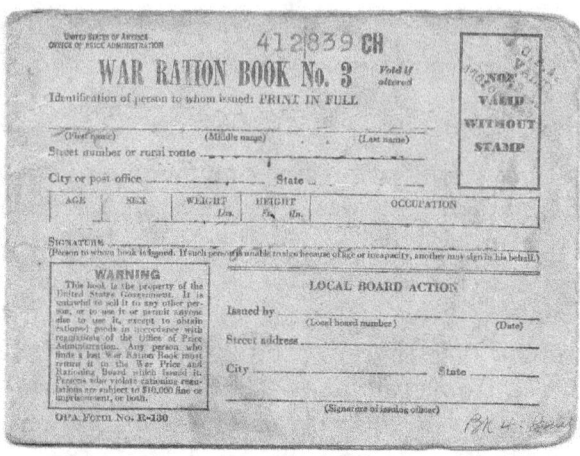

(From the Marie Sturdevant collection)
Images of the front and back covers of War Ration Book 3, and
ration stamps from War Ration Books 3 and 4.

Butter was one of the food items rationed during the war, and in its place, people used oleomargarine, a spread made from vegetable oils. Margarine was introduced to Americans in the late 1800's. It soon became a less expensive alternative to butter. Because of its natural white color, an artificial yellow dye was mixed in by the manufacturer to give a more appealing appearance. The American dairy industry felt threatened by the competition of this low-cost spread and responded by lobbying their politicians to put a ban on margarine. In 1886, Congress passed the Margarine Act, which imposed higher taxes and annual fees on margarine manufacturers. By 1902, thirty-two states, particularly the dairy states, passed laws banning the sale of yellow margarine. During this time, the margarine manufacturers found a way around the color ban and began packaging capsules containing yellow dye along with the white spread for a do it yourself coloring. This practice continued through World War II. There are many stories about mixing the capsule of yellow dye into the white margarine when sharing memories of life on the home front during the war, but in fact this wasn't unique to those years. The sale of margarine increased during the war since butter was a rationed food item. Because you needed a red stamp to purchase butter, which was also the stamp needed for meats, consumers used less butter.

My mom would tell me stories about mixing the little capsule of yellow dye into the margarine, but it just didn't have the same taste of butter. My mother-in-law shared stories about how she and her siblings would fight over who would mix the yellow dye into the white spread. I have also heard stories that it was difficult to mix the yellow dye into the hard, white margarine. One person shared how her hands hurt from kneading the dye into the margarine.

The OPA warned people, "never to buy rationed goods without ration stamps, and never pay more than the legal price." These words were written on the back of War Ration Book 4. However, rationing resulted in illegal activity known as the Black Market, involving the sale of goods outside the restrictions and guidelines established by the OPA. In the United States, the Black Market profiteers dealt mainly with the sale of sugar, meat and gasoline. As long as there were people willing to pay the higher prices, the Black Market would flourish through the war years.

One of the ways that people could reduce the negative impact of food rationing was to grow their own vegetables. The farmers had to concern themselves with providing food for the soldiers, and as a result there was less produce for people on the home front. Victory Gardens were grown in backyards and sometimes on open lots in neighborhoods where several families would pool their resources. This was another way that people felt they were making a contribution to the war effort as well as keeping themselves busy while loved ones were serving in the military.

For the women of the 1930's and 1940's, sheer hosiery was part of the fashion. An outfit was not complete without the finished look of sheer stockings. Nylon and silk were the most common materials used for hosiery, but these were also essential materials used in the war effort. Nylon was strong and light-weight, and for that reason it was useful in making tents, parachutes, and rope. Silk was the best material for making gun powder sacks. Because of the need for these materials for the war effort, drives were held to collect nylon and silk stockings and eventually these materials became less available for women's hosiery. My mom described to me how women would apply leg makeup and sometimes paint a dark line up the back of the leg to give the illusion of stockings. She considered it to be more of a bother. My dad commented on this practice of using leg makeup in one of his letters to my mom.

(Excerpts from my dad's letters from here forward will be presented in bold italics and indented.)

> ***You're not kidding when you say that putting on leg make up is silly. I should think it would be easier to put on your stockings every day instead of trying to paint that stuff on. But I suppose you girls are all the same when it comes to fashion.***

> ### Lowry Field, July 23, 1942

Other rationed items were tires, gasoline, automobiles, bicycles, fuels and shoes. Some materials and goods were in short supply because they were needed for the war effort, while others were less available because they were imported from countries we were at war with or countries that were occupied by the enemy. One such material in short supply for both reasons was rubber. Most of the rubber imported by the U.S. came from the Dutch East Indies which was occupied by the Japanese. Rubber as well as steel and other metals were necessary for manufacturing weapons, ammunition and other war supplies. Junk rallies or scrap drives were promoted as a way of recycling these materials for use in manufacturing supplies needed for the war. Even children were involved by collecting scraps of metal and rubber in their little red wagons. My father-in-law remembered having an occasional afternoon off from school and going around the neighborhood to collect various scraps and discarded items. He told me how he used to save the inner foil wrapping from his gum and roll several pieces of the foil into a larger ball which eventually would be added to the scrap pile. Written on the back of War Ration Book 4 was, "When you have used your ration, salvage the tin cans and waste fats. They are needed to make munitions for our fighting men. Cooperate with your local Salvage Committee." I remember my mom telling me how she used to save the fat from bacon and meats. These waste fats were collected in tin cans and returned to the grocer or butcher. Waste fats were used in making glycerin. This was a necessary ingredient in making gun powder and nitroglycerin.

Early in 1942, voluntary gasoline rationing was encouraged, but was quickly seen as ineffective. In May of 1942, mandatory rationing began on the east coast. By the end of the year, gasoline rationing was extended across the whole country. It was reasoned that if gasoline was rationed, it would save on the rubber necessary for tires, because it would limit the number of automobiles on the road, and therefore the wear and tear on the tires. A person had to file an application with the local OPA for gasoline ration stamps and a window sticker for their car. In 1942, the OPA established *The Idle Tire Purchase Plan*. You could be denied gasoline ration stamps if you possessed more than five tires. There were different types of stamps and window stickers depending on need to travel. Most people had "A Stickers," which allowed you to buy three to four gallons of gasoline per week. The green "B Stickers" were for people whose transportation was deemed necessary for the war effort. They were allowed eight gallons per week. The red "C Stickers" were designated for other professions, such as ministers, physicians and mail carriers. The "T Stickers" were for truck drivers who had access to an unlimited supply of gasoline, although records were kept of how much gasoline they used. A unit from the ration card had to be turned in when purchasing gasoline. The attendant at the station needed to present the units to their distributors in order to replenish their supply of gasoline. The government also established a mandatory speed limit of thirty-five miles per hour, called the Victory Speed Limit.

(From the Preston Sturdevant, Jr. collection)
The front and back of a gasoline ration card

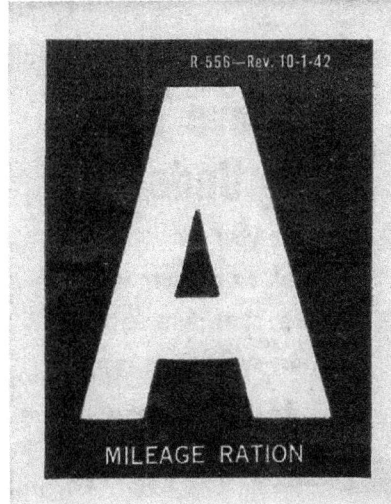

(From the Marie Sturdevant collection)
Image of the front and back of an "A Sticker"

People were no longer allowed to use their automobiles for pleasure driving. Public transportation and car pooling were among the ways to get around. While my dad was stationed at the various bases in New England, he was able to get home once in a while, but transportation wasn't always the easiest.

> *I hope that my father has my car fixed for me for when I get home next time, because I'm sick of riding on the buses. They say that you can't use your cars for pleasure driving anymore, but I've heard that the soldiers can, so that's why I hope it's fixed.*

Westover Field, Massachusetts, January 10, 1943

The home front contributed greatly to the outcome of the war. Doing with less was something most Americans were used to because they had lived with less during the Great Depression. Now there were limited goods because so many things were needed to keep the troops supplied. In addition to food and materials, the war needed funding. Another way Americans could contribute to the war effort was to purchase war bonds issued by the U.S. government.

These debt securities, which financed the military operations during war time, yielded a rate below the market value. Even so, purchasing war bonds appealed to the patriotic spirit as people felt they were helping to fund the war.

Before the United States entered the war at the end of 1941, preparations were being made for war-related emergencies. The war department began building its Army and Navy. The first peace-time draft in U.S. history took place on October 16, 1940. This act of compulsory military service came in response to Nazi Germany's conquest of France in the spring of 1940. All males between the ages of twenty-one and thirty-six were required to register for the draft, and a lottery system was used to determine who would be called to service. The first lottery was October 29, 1940. The length of time for military service was twelve months. Once the U.S. was drawn into the war in December of 1941, the age of the draftees was expanded to include all males between the ages of eighteen and forty-five. The length of service was also increased to the duration of the war plus six months. Men who didn't pass their physical examination were deemed unfit for military service and given deferments. Some who were in critical professions deemed essential on the home front were also exempt from military service.

A number of other defense measures were enacted by Congress including the raising of taxes and increasing the national debt limit. In May 1941, the U.S. Office of Civil Defense was established. Since the leaders in Washington were concerned about the limited resources available to conduct a war, a plan was needed to ensure that these precious resources were not taken away for an unlikely attack on U.S. soil. By empowering U.S. citizens to defend their own neighborhoods, people at home felt safer and more involved in the war. Out of fear of enemy attack on the home front, the civil defense conducted air raid drills and blackouts. People who were outside were instructed to take cover. If you were inside your home, you had to pull your shades and keep light inside at a minimum. The reason for this was to make populated areas less visible to enemy planes that might fly overhead. Air raid wardens would walk through neighborhoods and check for non-compliance, such as light showing through a crack in a window shade and even the glow from a lighted cigarette. My father-in-law told stories about being an air raid messenger during the war. He wore an arm band to signify his role. In the darkness of an ongoing air raid drill, his job was to carry messages from one place to another. He remembered one of those dark nights, having to ride his bike along the road, hitting the curb and flying off his bike and onto the pavement. My mother-in-law remembered being frightened by the sound of the air raid siren. Over time, though, the drills became rather routine and she and her family went through the motions just to comply with the rules and regulations. My mom wrote to my dad about the air raid drills, dim-outs and blackouts. He commented about his experience:

> *We haven't had any blackouts at all here in Denver yet that I know of. In Miami they have a dim out every night. The cars have to drive with their dim lights only, and the street lights are painted black on the side facing the ocean.*

Lowry Field, Colorado, August 1, 1942

(From the Marie Sturdevant collection)
WWII Blue Star Banner

There were signs of war and those serving our country as you passed through almost any neighborhood in America during WWII. Hanging in the front window of many homes were banners symbolizing the service of a member of the family. These blue star banners, also called son in service banners, or mother's window banners, were a reminder of the countless numbers of men fighting in the war. This symbolic flag of a blue star on a white field with red trim, originated during the first world war. There was a sad reminder of sacrifice when a blue star was replaced with a gold star which signified that the family's loved one was killed in the war.

Communication between the home front and those serving in the military was essential in keeping up the morale. Letter writing was encouraged as a way of giving emotional support to the men and women serving in places far away from home. Civilians were encouraged to write about normal routines, life at home and family events. Wartime romances developed and were kept alive through the frequent exchanges of letters.

(From the H. Virginia Sandstrom collection)
This envelope displays the phrase which came to be equated with censorship in letter writing during WWII, "Idle Gossip Sinks Ships." The censor stamp with the initials of the person who read the letter is seen in the lower left hand corner.

Letter writing increased as did the space needed to transport the mail back and forth between the home front and battle front. In order to save on this precious cargo space which was also needed to transport military supplies, a system of letter writing was devised which would decrease the amount of space needed for the bags of mail. Victory Mail, or V-Mail, used a specially designed letter-sheet. The address of the recipient was written at the top of the sheet and the letter was written in the space below, and limited one's writing to a single page. Like all mail sent during the war, V-Mail had to pass through a censor before being processed through a photograph machine and transferred onto microfilm. The rolls of microfilm were sent to a destination close to the addressee. A photograph of the original letter was made and delivered to the intended recipient. V-Mail letters were sent postage free by members of the military, while others pre-paid at the domestic rate of three cents regular mail and six cents for air mail. This system of using V-Mail reduced the amount of space for bags of mail by over 90 per cent.

V-Mail Service provides the most expeditious dispatch and reduces the weight of mail to and from personnel of our Armed Forces outside the continental United States. When addressed to points where micro-film equipment is operated, a miniature photographic negative of the message will be made and sent by the most expeditious transportation available for reproduction and delivery. The original message will be destroyed after the reproduction has been delivered. Messages addressed to or from points where micro-film equipment is not operated will be transmitted in their original form by the most expeditious means available.

INSTRUCTIONS

(1) Write the entire message plainly on the other side within marginal lines.

(2) PRINT the name and address in the two panels provided. Addresses to members of the Armed Forces should include rank or rating of the addressee, unit to which attached, and APO or Naval address.

(3) Fold, seal, and deposit in any post office letter drop or street letter box.

(4) Enclosures must not be placed in this envelope and a separate V-Mail letter must be sent if you desire to write more than one sheet.

(5) V-Mail letters may be sent free of postage by members of the Armed Forces. When sent by others postage must be prepaid at domestic rates (3c ordinary mail, 6c if air mail is desired).

POST OFFICE DEPARTMENT PERMIT NO 14

(From the H. Virginia Sandstrom collection)
Instructions found on the back of specially designed letter-sheet
used in V-mail letter writing.

V-Mail had its limitations since pictures and newspaper clippings could not be enclosed, nor could it carry the scent of a familiar perfume. For this reason, V-Mail, despite its patriotic intent, was not very popular. Most people still sent regular first class mail. Like many others, my dad didn't like V-Mail, and preferred longer letters.

About your writing all your letters V-Mail, I wish you wouldn't. Of course they're all right, but I'd much rather get long Air Mail letters instead. That is if you don't mind. After all, who am I to tell you what kind of letters to write? As long as I get them though, I'm satisfied. I'd rather get mail than eat, and you know how I like to eat.

Finschhafen, New Guinea, December 26, 1943

Well I didn't receive a letter from you today, so I'll answer the other one that I got yesterday. I hope to hear from you again tomorrow. If I don't, you're going to get another V-Mail - so there too! No kidding though, I do hope I hear from you again tomorrow. The more I hear from you, the better I like it.

Saidor, New Guinea, March 29, 1944

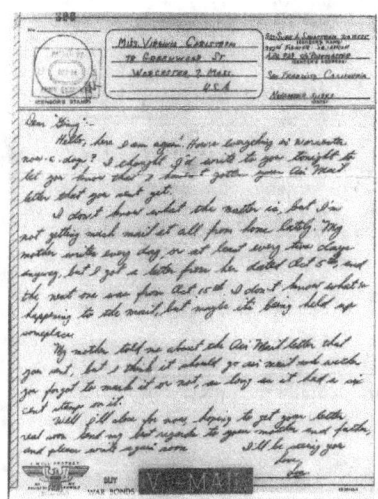

(From the H. Virginia Sandstrom collection)

On the left is the final reproduction of a correspondence sent by V-mail. The reproduction is about one quarter of the size of the original hand-written letter, (4" x 5"). In the upper left hand corner is the censor stamp. The reproduced image of the letter was folded and placed in an envelope measuring 4 ½" x 3 ½".

It was extremely important to keep sensitive strategic information of the troops a secret from the enemy. For this reason, letters were censored. "Loose Lips Sink Ships" was a phrase commonly used during WWII. Anything that might reveal the strength of the troops, including location, would be literally cut out of a letter. Signs of low morale among the troops that might be exploited by the enemy could also be detected by the censors. Enlisted men's letters were censored by the officers, or sometimes the chaplain.

> *I can't tell you how close or how far I am to the front, because the censor would cut it out anyway. In fact a new order came through so we can't even tell where we are now. All we can say is that we're somewhere in the Western Pacific.*

Port Moresby, New Guinea, September 29, 1943

> *I'll be able to tell you these things about where I've been and what I've seen, etc., etc., after the war is over. Until then though, we have censorship regulations to comply with.*

Saidor, New Guinea, April 4, 1944

The rules of censorship changed throughout the war and at times became more lenient.

> *Remember in my last letter I told you that we're not allowed to say exactly where we are, or where we have been? Well they just came out with new censorship regulations, and now we can tell where we've been, but we still can't give our exact present location. It seems funny that they should come out with that, right after I got through telling you that we couldn't write about it. I guess they're getting a little more lenient in their censorship rules now. We can't tell you when we were at the different places, or the order in which we were there, but you don't*

want to mind that.

Luzon, Philippine Islands, April 6, 1945

As the war in the Pacific approached it's dramatic conclusion in the summer of 1945, censorship rules tightened up again. In an undated letter, (the envelope is postmarked July 17, 1945), from "Somewhere in the Western Pacific," my dad wrote:

> *Dear "Ginny,"*
>
> *- I'm sorry I haven't written for the past few days, but as you can see, my address has changed again. It is now A.P.O. 245. We're not allowed to say where we are, and we can't even put any dates on our letters, but they'll probably let up on the censorship rules pretty soon.*

A.P.O. (Army Post Office) numbers were another way to ensure anonymity of location. A letter from home would be sent to a stateside address with an A.P.O. number which represented the overseas location where the soldier was stationed. As the troops moved from one location to another, the A.P.O. number would change. Because of the troops being on the move, sometimes it would take a long time for letters and packages to reach the recipient. Days might pass when no letters would be received and then on a later day, the mail would finally catch up and several letters would be in the mail call. At times the letters would not be received in the order they were sent.

> *Well, I finally received some mail from you. I got four of them, but I'm going to answer them one at a time. I got ten letters the day before yesterday, and I got eighteen yesterday. Boy, am I going to have a job trying to answer them all. I'll have writer's cramp before I'm through. I get writer's cramp just writing out my address because it's so long!*

Finschhafen, New Guinea, February 27, 1944

Our mail doesn't always get here in the order that you send them. This letter I am answering now was written Jan. 24, and I've already had mail from you for February. Oh well, what do I care, as long as I hear from you, and the oftener the better.

Saidor, New Guinea, March 13, 1944

I hope I get some more [letters] from you soon. We haven't had any mail here now for five days, so we should be getting a bunch of it soon. You don't mind missing mail a day once in a while, but when it stretches out to five days, then that's too much. Oh well, that's the way it goes, and I don't suppose there's anything that can be done about it.

Saidor, New Guinea, April 19, 1944

As if it weren't bad enough that letters could be held up for days or weeks, packages would sometimes be delayed for longer periods of time and possibly be received damaged. My dad wrote about the condition of some of the packages sent from home

Well I finally received two more of my Christmas packages yesterday, but they sure were a mess. Out of the two boxes that I got, all I could salvage was a package of Beech-Nut gum. One package was from Harry Steemson's folks, and the other one was from one of my mother's friends in Auburn, Mrs. Hanson. There were a couple of nice big fruit cakes, a nice home-baked chocolate cake, and some cookies, candy, and cigarettes that had to be thrown away because they were all getting moldy. The packages were all squashed, and I guess they must have gotten wet at one time too. It's really a shame the way some of the packages get over here, but I guess there's nothing we can do about it. I hate to write to them and tell them how the packages were spoiled. I suppose I could tell them that they got here in good condition and that everything tasted good, but I don't believe that would be the right thing to say. I know they'll feel bad about it when I tell them, but I'd much rather tell the truth than to lie about it. I was looking at the postmarks, and they were mailed last September. That means they've been on the way for six months - a half year! That's an awful long time for a package to get here, but I suppose the way we were moving around so much at the time, accounted for it. Oh well, I hope the rest of my packages get here in fairly decent condition anyway.

Luzon, Philippine Islands, March 5, 1945

Just as it would sometimes take several days to receive letters from home, letters from overseas would sometimes be delayed which could create anxiety for family at home.

I'm sorry you didn't hear from me for over three weeks there, but I was busy and everything, and it couldn't be helped. My folks didn't hear from me for two weeks at one time, and they say my mother was really worried. I write to her practically every night so I don't know why they didn't hear from me for so long. She worries a lot when she doesn't hear from me but I tell her not to, because sometimes the mail gets held up for a while. I guess she worries because she loves me. (ahem)

Leyte, Philippine Islands, January 10, 1945

My dad sent over 200 regular air mail letters and several V-Mails to my mom while serving in the Army Air Corps. His letters described what life was like on the bases and in the jungles of the Western Pacific Islands of New Guinea, the Philippines and Ryukyu Islands.

The days were long and unbearably hot as he and the armament crews loaded bombs and synchronized machine guns on the planes, while watching their pilots bombing and strafing the enemy a short distance away. Naval destroyers could be seen up the coast, shelling the Japanese, while field artillery guns were heard going off throughout the day. Sleep was often interrupted by the sound of the air raid siren when bombing raids were carried out against the Allied airstrips where the squadron was stationed. My dad and his buddies would jump out of their bunks and take cover in their foxholes in the darkness of night. Their tents and bunks were built on the ground which became very damp as it rained almost every night during the rainy season. Sometimes the men in his squadron were able to secure the wood needed to build a rough floor in the tent, but then it wouldn't be long before they were on the move again. There were times when he wouldn't hear anything from home because the mail was held up as they moved from one location to another. These delays would stretch days into an eternity of anticipation as communications from home could take weeks and even months to reach my dad and others serving overseas while they were on the move.

My dad's letters would often describe the ways the members of his squadron would entertain themselves during off-duty hours. But mostly, he expressed his desire for the war to end and to be able to come home and settle into a normal life again.

Most of his letters ended the same way....

Well I guess I'll close for this time, hoping to hear from you again real soon. Send my best regards to your mother and father.

I'll be seeing you
all my love
Joe.

Basic Training and
Preparing For Overseas Deployment
June 1942 - May 1943

On June 18, 1942, my dad began active service with the United States Army at Fort Devens in Massachusetts. Fort Devens served as a reception center for men from New England, who were drafted into military service. Following a few days of initial processing at Devens, my dad was transferred to a replacement center in Miami, Florida. Unlike other centers for basic training, where the recruits were quartered in barracks, Miami quartered the recruits in hotels.

In his first letter since entering the service my dad wrote about his trip to Miami and the first few days at the replacement training center.

> *We left Fort Devens on Tuesday, June 23, at 4:30 P.M. We rode on a Pullman car, and we were on that train for fifty three hours, without getting off once. We arrived here Thursday night. I'm sorry I haven't written before, but I haven't had much time to myself yet. We've had clothing checkups and physicals, and I.Q.'s and everything else to take up our time.*

War in the Pacific Timeline

December 7, 1941:

The Japanese attacked Pearl Harbor drawing the United States into the war in the Pacific. The Japanese also launched attacks on Malaya, Hong Kong, Guam, the Philippine Islands, Wake Island, and Midway Island.

February 19, 1942

President Roosevelt issued Executive Order 9066, authorizing the relocation of thousands of American citizens of Japanese ancestry to internment camps.

March 8-10, 1942:

The Japanese invaded New Guinea and landed troops at Finschhafen, securing their hold on the northern coastline.

So far the Army has been swell. We have regular hours, and regular meals. We get up at 5:30 A.M., and get to bed at 10:00 P.M. except on Saturday, when we can stay up until 11:00 P.M. As you can see from my address, I'm in the Air Forces now, and boy does that make me happy.

Boy are we living in class down here! I'm on the seventh floor of a twelve story hotel in a front room. It's two blocks from the beach, and you get to see the beach and the ocean from my room. We have three fellows to a room and my two roommates are swell. One of them is a 'Swede' and his name is Jacobson. We talk Swedish to each other once in a while and we have everybody else crazy trying to find out what we're saying;
(even we don't know half of the time.)

Miami Replacement Training Center, June 27, 1942

In the first few weeks of basic training, much of the time was spent drilling in the hot Florida sun, and taking tests in preparation for more advanced training.

It sure does get hot down here, and I do mean __HOT__. We go out to drill and I get soaking wet with sweat. Sometimes the sun can be shining and it can start raining at the same time. When it rains down here it really rains. If we happen to be out drilling when it starts to rain, we keep on drilling whether we like it or not.

Miami Replacement Training Center, June 23, 1942

There was a need to prepare recruits to be sent to technical schools and specialized training as quickly as possible. Physical conditioning was at the heart of basic training, but the time was also used to determine where the recruits would be best suited after their initial few weeks in the service.

We had to have five I.Q.'s down here so that they could find out what we were best suited for when they send us to school. We had our choice of twenty different schools that we could go to. I picked out the airplane armor school. That teaches us all about the machine guns, cannons, and bombs on the airplane. We have to see that they are kept in proper working condition, and that they are supplied with enough ammunition. I'm not certain, but I think that this school is in Denver, Colorado. We have to have our basic training down here first, then we go to wherever the school is. The school lasts for fifteen weeks. We are supposed to get a ten or fourteen day furlough when we finish school, but that won't be for a few months yet. I'll be glad when we get our furlough, because I would like to go home and see the old gang again.

After I've been in the Army for three months, I can apply for Officer's Training School, because the marks on my I.Q.'s were high enough to make me eligible. I don't know how they mark the tests, but we have to have a mark of 110 or better to be eligible for it, and my lowest mark was 114. My highest mark was 144. Boy, I was happy when I heard that.

March 1942

Reports of Japanese atrocities against allied prisoners of war and indigenous people began to emerge. These included acts of rape, murder and horrific torture.

April 10, 1942

After surrendering to the Japanese following a three month battle in the Philippine province of Bataan, approximately 76,000 American and Filipino prisoners were forced into a three day, seventy mile march, characterized by severe physical abuse and murder. The prisoners had to march in the scorching heat with little food and water. Some prisoners were beaten, beheaded or bayoneted during this torturous march. The Bataan Death March was later judged by an Allied military commission to be a Japanese war crime.

It gets pretty lonesome down here in one way, because none of my friends are here. I've met a swell bunch of fellows though, and we get along good together. Everyone in my squadron comes from Devens, and most of them are from Massachusetts. Boy it's really beautiful, and it's also very romantic; that's why I wish you were down here too. There has been a full moon since we got here, and when that shines down through the palm trees, it sure makes a beautiful picture.

I have to go on guard duty tonight and I want to get some rest. I'll be on duty from two o'clock until four o'clock in the morning, so you can imagine how much sleep I'll get tonight.

Don't forget to write now.
Love,
Lou
P.S. I'll "Keep 'Em Flying," if you keep the production line going at Norton Co.

Miami Replacement Training Center, July 5, 1942

"KEEP 'EM FLYING"

In early July 1942, my dad was transferred to Lowry Field in Denver Colorado where he began his training in the Armament Division of the U.S. Army Air Corps Technical School. He arrived sometime around July 13.

AIR CORPS TECHNICAL SCHOOL
LOWRY FIELD. COLORADO

He described what a typical day at Lowry Field was like. Between school and drilling, his day was full from around 4:00 A.M. until evening.

We get up at 4:05 A.M. and wash, brush our teeth, shave, make up our bunks, and sweep and mop out the barracks. Then we march to breakfast, and after that we march to school so that we're there for 6:00 A.M. We go to dinner at 11:00 A.M. and go back to school at 12:00 noon. We get through school at 2:00 and then march back to our barracks. We fall out for our calisthenics (physical exercises), at 2:15 , and finish at 3:00 P.M. After that we have to run around a 3/4 mile track. We go to supper at 4:30 P.M. and after that we have the rest of the night to ourselves. We have our studying to do too, so that takes up more of our time. The lights go out in our barracks at 8:30 P.M. and we have to be in bed at 9:00 P.M. On Saturdays though, we can go wherever we want to after our calisthenics, as long as we are back at camp by 9:00 P.M. on Sunday night. I think they are trying to wear us out instead of build us up.

Lowry Field, August 7, 1942

April 18, 1942

Sixteen specially modified U.S. B-25 Mitchell bombers, led by Colonel James Doolittle left the deck of the U.S.S. Hornet, Destination: Tokyo. This first U.S. assault on mainland Japan during WWII, lifted the American morale which was very low since the attack on Pearl Harbor. Eight crew members were taken prisoner by the Japanese. Most of the B-25 crews landed in China where they were aided by Chinese civilians and soldiers. Out of gratitude for their assistance, the Americans gave gifts to the Chinese who aided them after the raid. However, the Chinese paid dearly for their efforts. Atrocities were carried out on those carrying American items. An estimated 250,000 Chinese were killed by the Japanese while searching for Doolittle's men.

I've finished two parts of the course that I am taking now, and I've started on the third. The first part was "Chemical Warfare," and the second part was "Explosives and Ammunition." Now I am studying about "Small Arms" which deals with pistols, rifles, shot guns, and machine guns. I had a final exam on each of my first two courses and my marks were 96%, and 95%. Not bad, eh? The courses are getting tougher as they go along though, so I guess I'll have to start studying a little harder.

Lowry Field, August 1, 1942

In one of his letters, my dad wrote about .30 caliber machine guns, and his experience at the malfunction laboratory:

We were out to the Malfunction Laboratory today. They had sixteen guns there, and we had to try and fire every one of them. They all had something wrong with them, and we were supposed to tell what it was by trying to fire them. Some of them would fire and some of them wouldn't. They divided the class into groups, with two in each group. Each group had one gun at a time, and we had to go around to every gun, and pick out what was wrong with them. We had to tell what was wrong with them by the positions in which the gun stopped, and how the gun reacted. Then we had to write an analysis of what went on inside the gun to make it work like it did. The hard part of it was that we couldn't look inside the gun to see what was the matter with it. One fellow hurt his hand on one of the guns because he didn't know enough to keep it out of the way. This gun fires about 1350 rounds per minute, or about 22 rounds per second, so you can imagine how fast the gun is going back and forth. You might not think that it's possible for a gun to fire that fast, well neither did any of us until we went to that laboratory today and found out for ourselves by firing them.

Lowry Field, August 20, 1942

(From the H. Virginia Sandstrom collection)
A postcard my dad sent to my mom on October 28, 1942

In addition to school and drilling, the enlisted men had other assignments. K.P., which stands for kitchen patrol or kitchen police, was assigned out of necessity and not as a punishment, as some civilians thought. K.P. could be monotonous as the days were long and the duties consisted of tasks associated with a military mess, including food preparation, serving food in a chow line, table cleanup, dish washing, and floor mopping.

I was on K.P. I didn't do anything wrong to get it, it's just because everybody gets a crack at it. I had it once at Devens, once in Miami, and five times here in Lowry Field. The reason I had it as much here is because we were here for a week before we started school, and they couldn't bear to see us hanging around not doing anything, so they put us on K.P. to keep us busy. And I do mean they kept us busy; from 4:30 A.M. to 7:00 P.M. Boy what a long day that makes. When you get to the barracks at about 7:15 P.M., you're ready to go to sleep.

Lowry Field, August 10, 1942

There was time for rest and recreation when not studying, drilling or attending classes. He wrote about some of the ways they entertained themselves during their off hours.

Here we have two day rooms. One where we can read, write or listen to the radio, and the other where we can play pool or ping pong and also listen to the radio. We can also play softball, baseball, football, volleyball, or pitch horseshoes, so you can see how we have plenty to do. We have a service club where there is a library and a place to study. You ought to see the radio we have in there. It is a combination radio and phonograph, presented to us by none other than, <u>Glenn Miller</u>.

Lowry Field, July 23, 1942

In late August, my dad expressed his frustration with moving to a different barracks

Dear "Ginny," -

Please excuse me for not writing before this, but I've been awfully busy. Believe it or not, <u>I've moved</u>

38

again. I'm still in Lowry Field, but I moved to a different squadron, and a different barracks. Boy was I mad when I heard that we were going to move again. Now it will take about a week or more to get straightened out on my mail again. We got home from school yesterday and they told us that we were going to move. It took us the rest of the day to move our stuff over to the other barracks and get things straightened out. The reason we moved was because they wanted to separate the 'A' shift from the 'B' shift. I'm the 'A' shift and we lost the coin toss, so we were the unlucky ones that had to move. In case you were wondering, the difference between the 'A' and 'B' shifts is that we go to school from 6:00 AM to 2:00 PM, while the 'B' shift goes from 2:00 PM to 10:00 PM. I suppose we'll just about get settled over here now, and then we'll be shipped to another field, because I've only got six more weeks left of school now. Well, that's how it is in the Army; we're never in one place long enough to get really settled. You probably know that as well as I do now on account of all the different changes of addresses that I've had since I came in the Army, and that's only a little over two months now.

Lowry Field, August 28, 1942

The weekends were a time to get away from the routine of school, drilling and military life. Sometimes my dad would use a weekend pass to go into town, and other times he would take a trip to the mountains with some of his buddies.

We went up to the mountains again yesterday. We went up to Squaw Mountain, and that is a little over 11,000 ft. high. We had to stop the car and hike for two miles to get to the top. It was a long and tiresome climb, but it was well worth it. They had a lookout tower at the very top, and we went up to that. The leaves are starting to turn colors now, and you can imagine how beautiful it looked. It's so beautiful that there aren't any words to describe it.

Lowry Field, September 21, 1942

In some of his letters my dad would mention friends from back home who were in the service, and looking forward to seeing them when he would finish school and get a furlough. His closest friends were Gus, Russell, and Harry. As the time came closer when he would be shipping out to a new field, he knew there was a chance he might get home for a visit and see the old gang. When he was only a week away from graduation he wrote about wishing to see his friend Gus.

I'd like to be home for Gussie's party because I probably won't see him for quite a while now. Well, I'll be there mentally anyway, even if I can't be there physically, and wish him all the luck in the world, wherever he may go. I've said it before, but I'll say it again, that I hope he gets into the Air Corps, and that we get around to seeing each other sometime, someplace, soon.

We had a personal inspection yesterday. We had to put on our dress uniforms, and get out and stand in the hot sun for about an hour while the general walked up and down the ranks to see how we looked. We had to have a clean shave, haircut, shoes shined, and cleaned and pressed uniform. It wasn't too bad though because we got out of doing our calisthenics. I guess we made up for it today though, because first of all we had to do our exercises, then we had to run over the 'obstacle course,' then, as if that wasn't bad enough, we had to run around the track. When we got through with that, we had to move, so we had a pretty busy day today.

Lowry Field, September 24, 1942

By the end of September, as graduation was getting closer, he began writing about where he might be transferred.

When we go to our next field from here, some of us will train for overseas, and some of us will stay here in the U.S. at some Coast Patrol. Well I'm not going to worry about where I'm going, because that remains to be seen. It doesn't make any difference where I go anyway, because I'll still have a tough job. In case you didn't know it, it's not so easy to install and synchronize machine guns, and load bombs on planes, etc.

Lowry Field, September 28, 1942

On October 2, 1942, my dad graduated from the Air Force Technical School. He remained stationed at Lowry Field for a couple of weeks until orders came through where he would be transferred.

When we ship out of here, we won't all go to the same place, so that's why we had the banquet last night. Some of us probably won't ever see each other again after we leave here, while some of us will go together. I hope that most of us go together,

41

August 7-8, 1942

Units of the 1st Marine Division landed on Guadalcanal in the Solomon Islands in the first major U.S. offensive operation of the war in the Pacific.

September 12-14, 1942

After two days of fierce fighting by U.S. Marines at "Bloody Ridge" on Guadalcanal, the Japanese commander, General Kawaguchi ordered his men to retreat.

October 26, 1942

In the Battle of Santa Cruz, off Guadalcanal, Japanese warships inflicted serious damage to the U.S.S Enterprise and destroyed the U.S.S. Hornet.

because they are a swell bunch of fellows. I don't know if we can get off the field this weekend or not. They usually take the passes away from the graduates in case they are to be shipped in a hurry.

Lowry Field, October 3, 1942

My dad continued writing letters from Lowry Field for the couple of weeks following graduation. His days were filled with anticipation of being transferred closer to home, and monotonous hours of K.P.

The way things look here now, we'll be here a week before we ship out. Of course I don't know for sure, but the class that graduated ahead of us had a week of K.P. before they shipped out. Some of them are still here, but I think they're going out tomorrow. I was talking to some of the fellows before they left, and they were going to Westover Field, Mass, La Guardia Field, N.Y., Conn., N.J., Utah, and California, so you can see that they're shipping them all over the country. I hope that they send me to Mass., Conn., or N.Y. because then I'll be able to go home for the weekends. Most of the fellows were going where they'd be only three or four hours from their homes. I hope I'm as lucky as they are, but I suppose that remains to be seen.

Lowry Field, October 5, 1942

From the Sven L. Sandstrom collection)
My dad, sometime in the summer of 1942, Denver, Colorado.

From the Sven L. Sandstrom collection)
My dad and his friend, Kenny, Denver, Colorado, 1942.

From the Sven L. Sandstrom collection)
My dad, Private Sven L. Sandstrom is in the back row, fifth from the left.

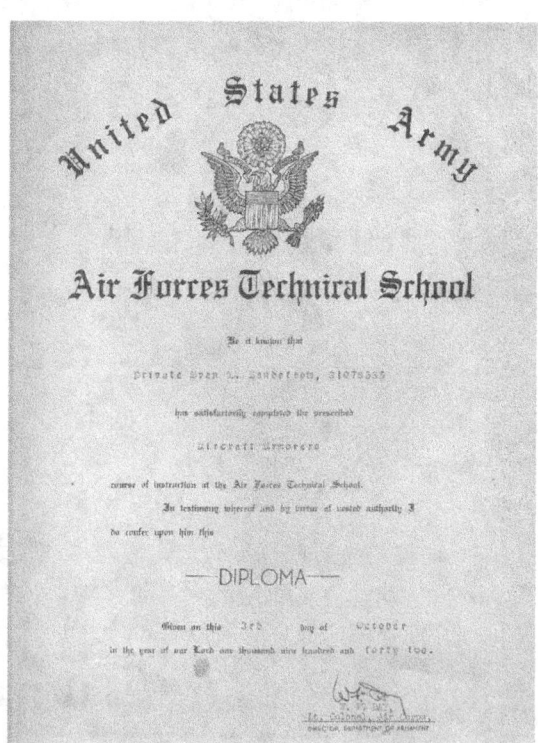

(From the Sven L. Sandstrom collection)
My dad's diploma from Army Air Force Technical School for Aircraft Armorer.

Well here it is Monday and I'm still here. Your letter just came today, and I was very glad to hear from you. I had K.P. on Tuesday, Thursday, and Saturday last week, and I had it again today. Yesterday the whole field had to parade in front of the general and a few more high ranking officers.

I still haven't made up my mind about what I am going to do. I don't know whether to try for Officers' School or just try for some stripes. I'll probably make up my mind someday though.

Lowry Field, October 12, 1942

Finally, orders came through and my dad was about to be shipped out to a base in New York. Once the orders came through, there was not the luxury of writing the usual long letters to home. In a brief letter he wrote:

Dear "Ginny," -

We just got word that we are being shipped today. I have to get all my junk together now, and get ready to go. I haven't got time to write anymore now because I haven't got much time to get ready. I'll write to you as soon as I get to my next field.

I'll be seeing you.
Love
Lou

Lowry Field, October 16, 1942

He arrived at Mitchell Field in Long Island, New York on Wednesday night October 21.

I arrived here Wednesday night. We didn't leave Denver until Monday instead of Friday as we were supposed to. Well now I've got some good news to tell you. We're going to ship out of here either tomorrow or Monday, and I'm going to Bradley Field in Windsor Locks, Conn. Just think, I'll only be about an hour and a half from home.

The Sergeant came around to us yesterday and he had a list of a few fields where they needed some armorers. He told us that we could take our pick of where we wanted to go.

I was the second one to see the list, so I told him to put me down for Conn. right away. They wanted one fellow for Westover Field in Chicopee, but I didn't want to go up there alone, so I took Bradley Field instead. There are about ten or twelve of us going up there.

November 14-15, 1942

U.S. and Japanese warships clashed off Guadalcanal. The U.S. Cruiser Juneau was sunk by a Japanese submarine. Five brothers, serving together aboard the Juneau were killed in the attack. The deaths of the five Sullivan brothers resulted in the U.S. War Department adopting "The Sole Survivor Policy." This policy was designed to protect surviving family members from the draft when a sibling or parent died in military service. This policy does not apply in times of war or national emergency.

February 9, 1943

Japanese resistance on Guadalcanal ended.

Mitchell Field, October 23, 1942

"The 348th Fighter Group began at Mitchell Field, New York on September 30, 1942, and was transferred to Bradley Field at Windsor Locks, Connecticut, on the same day. The first fighter squadron assigned to the group, the 342nd Fighter Squadron, was organized on October 4, 1942, at Bradley Field." [1]

---

[1] From *Kearby's Thunderbolts* © John Stanaway, Schiffer Publ. Ltd. and used by permission of the author. (Page 11).

My dad wrote about arriving at Bradley Field at Windsor Locks, Connecticut and for the first time, his return address included the Squadron to which he would be permanently assigned for the remainder of the war; the 342nd Fighter Squadron:

We arrived here at the field about half past two Sunday morning. We left New York at about 8:00 PM Saturday night.

I guess I'll start getting my stripes pretty soon now, because the Lieutenant said that there is plenty of chances for advancement, as long as we "keep our noses clean," and do what we're told.

The Squadron that I'm in is a new one, and they just started it a few weeks ago, so they haven't got any planes for us to work on yet. They're going to get some next month sometime. We'll be doing drill work, guard duty, and K.P. while we're waiting for the planes to come in. The K.P. won't be bad here though, because there's only about 150 men in our Squadron so far. Each Squadron has its own mess hall here, so we haven't got many men to feed.

Bradley Field, October 25, 1942

Only a couple of days later, my dad wrote about being moved again:

This is just a short note to let you know that <u>I'm moving again!</u> I know what you're thinking, but it isn't my fault that I have to move. My whole Squadron is moving out, so I have to go with them. I'll be a little closer to home anyway, because we are going up to Westover Field in Chicopee. I'll probably have to wait about a week or two for my mail now, if you've already answered my last letter, so I'll write to you as soon as I get settled in Westover Field, and then you can write to me again. They came around last night and told us about it, and we're going to leave around 9:00 AM this morning, (Wednesday - October 28).

Bradley Field, October 27, 1942

"On October 28, 1942, the 342nd Fighter Squadron moved to Westover Field, near Chicopee Falls, Massachusetts. By the next day, the Group was settled at Westover, where they were assigned their first P-47 Thunderbolt aircraft." [2]

March 2-4, 1943

U.S. defeated Japanese in the Battle of the Bismarck Sea.

April 21, 1943

President Roosevelt announced that the Japanese had executed captured airmen from the Doolittle Raid. The Japanese declared that captured Allied pilots would be given "one way tickets to hell."

May 15, 1943

The Australian hospital ship, HMAS Centuar was torpedoed and sunk by a Japanese submarine.

Fall 1942 - Early spring 1943

The newly organized 348th Fighter Group trained and made preparations for overseas deployment.

---

[2] From *Kearby's Thunderbolts* © John Stanaway, Schiffer Publ. Ltd. and used by permission of the author. (Page 11).

Once my dad settled in at Westover, he wrote about how he liked his new base and wished to stay in one place for a while since he had been doing a lot of moving. With each move, mail would be held up for a week or more.

> *I like it here in Westover Field, mainly because I'm so close to home. Now all I have to do is to get a pass so that I can get home. This is really a nice field here though, and it sure is big. I only hope that we stay here for a while now, so that I can get home once in a while. About getting home now, we don't get the weekends off like we've been getting at the other fields. We're only going to get off one day a week, and I don't know what day I'll get, because we haven't got our passes yet. When we get K.P. here, we get it three days at a time. My friend has had it for the past three days, and this is his last day for it. I just found out that I'm on it for the next three days, starting tomorrow. Isn't that something pleasant to look forward to?*

Westover Field, November 2, 1942

My dad finally had a day off where he was able to go home. When he returned to the base, he wrote a letter, where he expressed how he hated to leave home:

> *Boy how I hated to leave there last night. I guess I'm just one of them old fashioned home boys. I'll be glad when this war is over, so that I can get home again, because you don't know how much I miss you. I suppose I shouldn't be talking like this, but it's the truth.*

Westover Field, November 13, 1942

49

(From the Sven L. Sandstrom collection)
My dad and his brother Carl Albert sometime in the fall of 1942.

As time passed, the boredom of daily life on the base and waiting for overseas deployment was mixed with the desire for the war to end:

> *I just got a letter from one of my friends that I went to school with out in Denver. He's out in Wyoming now, and he expects to go "across" soon now. The way I feel now, I'd like to be with him and go across with him too. In fact everybody in my Squadron here feels that way now. We're getting sick of hanging around here every day in the week. I want either the war to stop so that I can go home again and stay there, or I want to go overseas.*

Westover Field, December 12, 1942

A few days later, he was shipped down to Bradley Field to work on some planes that were operating from that field.

Well I guess I won't be able to see you this week, because I was sent down here to Bradley Field in Conn. for a week, starting today. The reason I'm down here is because they sent a few of our planes down to operate from this field, and they needed some men to take care of them. I don't know why they're operating them from this field, but that's the Army for you. They picked Kenny and me and four other fellows from the Armament shop to come down here, besides the mechanics and radiomen, etc. I was kind of mad when I was told that I had to come down here, but there wasn't anything that I could do about it.

Bradley Field, December 16, 1942

As the war raged with fierce intensity throughout the world, the 342nd Fighter Squadron trained with the P-47 Thunderbolts. The ground crews were busy preparing planes for flight, while the pilots honed their skills in maneuvering the P-47's in target practice. "By early spring of 1943, six to ten fighter groups, including the 348th were equipped with the P-47 Thunderbolt and were destined for the war in Europe." [3]

The letters written in early 1943 often reflected the preparations that were being made for overseas deployment.

Now about my day off. Our pilots are starting target practice today, so that means that we'll have to clean guns on the planes every night, and I think they're going to need all of us here to help with that. I think our Sergeant will let at least one of us have a day off at a time though, so I'm going to ask him for Thursday night and Friday. We had a lot of work to do here today, because they brought down all the planes from our Squadron from Westover Field to

---

[3] From *Kearby's Thunderbolts* © John Stanaway, Schiffer Publ. Ltd. and used by permission of the author. (Page 15).

operate from here. They're not going to stay here all the time though. They only had them here for today. It's a good thing too, because we'll have enough work to keep us busy with the six planes that we've got here now that they're going to have target practice every day.

January 3, 1943

Our planes were out target practicing yesterday and today, so we had to work late to clean the guns. We got through fairly early last night. We got through at six-thirty. I came back to the barracks after that and cleaned up and went to bed. I was in bed by eight o'clock and I went right to sleep. Our ratings came out yesterday and Kenny and I were made Corporals. At least that's two stripes to my credit now, but I doubt if I'll get more now for a few months anyway. There are still quite a few more Corporals ahead of us to be made Sergeants first.

January 10, 1943

Sometime between January 10 and 17, the Squadron moved to Bedford Airdrome, Bedford, Massachusetts.

Well I've finally got time to catch up on my writing. As you can see by my address on the envelope, I've moved again. We've been kind of busy trying to get settled up here, and we're just about done now. We've still got a lot of work to do though, because this is a brand new field, and we're the only Squadron up here. We've been busy every minute of the day since we've been here, so I haven't had much time for writing or anything else. I'm Corporal of the Guard this week, so I'll have plenty of time for writing. I work from six o'clock at night until eight o'clock in the morning, and then I sleep during the day. My job as Corporal of the Guard this week is to see that guards are at their posts when they're supposed to be and see that they get relieved on time. I have a few hours to myself between the changes of guard, so I'll be able to answer all of my mail.

Bedford Airdrome, January 17, 1943

I got a letter from my mother today too, and she told me that Russell got his induction papers now, so he has to go to Fort Devens on Jan 26th, and he'll be inducted on Feb 2nd. If they have a party for him, I hope that I can get home for it. I missed Harry's and Gussie's, so I don't want to miss his if possible.

I've got to go out and change the guards in a few minutes now, so I'll continue the letter when I come back.

Well here I am back again, only I'm a little bit chilly now. Boy is it cold out tonight! There's an estimated sixty mile an hour wind, and it's almost ten below zero, so you can imagine how cold it is. Am I glad that I've got a fire in the stove in here to get me thawed out. The guards that just came off duty are just about frozen, and they're all going to sleep around the stove.

Bedford Airdrome, January 19,1943

As far as I know now, I'll be home for that dance up at the Auditorium on the 25th, unless something comes up in the meantime to prevent it. I hope not though, because I'd like to go to it.

I'm going to try to get a three day pass for around the first of March because Harry will be home then.

He's going to leave his camp two weeks from today, on the 28th. I'll bet he's awfully impatient waiting for that day to come. He'll probably be home around the 2nd or 3rd of March. It's sure going to be good to see him again after eight and one-half months. I hope that Gussie can get home too.

Bedford Airdrome, February 14, 1943

I was going to come home last Thursday like I told you I would, but a couple of the fellows came down with the measles, so they quarantined the whole camp. They were going to keep us in for twenty-one days, but nobody else got them, so they lifted the restriction on Friday afternoon. I was beginning to get mad when they told us that we were going to be quarantined for 21 days because I wouldn't have been able to get home for the dance this week, and I wouldn't have been able to get home to see Harry when he comes. I got a letter from Russell the other day, and he said that he likes it down in Miami Beach.

I had to work until 8:30 last night because I was in charge of the Alert Crew. We had to fix up four of our planes because they are being transferred to another Squadron. We got some of the newer P-47's to take their place.

Bedford Airdrome, February 23, 1943

My dad received a three day pass in early March and he was able to see his friends, Harry and Gus. Upon returning to the base, he wrote:

Well here I am back in camp again, a little bit tired after my three day pass. I was up until three and

(From the Sven L. Sandstrom collection)
My dad, Gus Tangring and Harry Steemson; March 7, 1943.

four o'clock every night when I was home. We were over to Harry's house every night playing the piano and singing. I was supposed to go back to the camp here on Saturday night, but I stayed over until Sunday night, because Gus came home for one day and I wanted to see him. Kenny was off on Saturday, so he stayed over the extra day with me too. Nobody missed us here, so they didn't say anything about our not being here. I wouldn't have cared if they did say anything anyway, because it was worth it to see Gus and Harry again after almost nine months. If Russell had been home then everything would have been complete. Speaking of Russell, he has left Miami Beach now, and I think he's on his way to Colorado, so as soon as I get his new address I'll send it to you.

I won't have any days off now for three weeks because I just had a three day pass, so I don't know when I'll see you again.

Bedford Airdrome, March 8, 1943

"The 348th received their orders for overseas shipment sometime in March. While it was originally planned that the 348th would be entering the war in Europe, things were heating up in the Pacific as the Fifth Air Force was trying to defend Port Moresby and prevent Japanese reinforcement in Northern New Guinea. General George Kenney's Fifth Air Force was outnumbered two to one, with worn-out fighters with limited range. The Operations Division of the War Department made the decision in late March to divert the 348th Fighter Group to the Fifth Air Force." [4]

The letters that my dad wrote were fewer and there was a shift in his mood. The last letter before deployment was dated March 28, 1943.

---

[4] From *Kearby's Thunderbolts* © John Stanaway, Schiffer Publ. Ltd. and used by permission of the author. (Page 16)

The next letter after that was written and sent from New Guinea on September 29, 1943. (It was sometime between those dates that my dad was promoted to the rank of Sergeant, as reflected in his return address in September.)

In his last letter written before shipping out he wrote about going home a couple of nights but not wanting to go out anyplace. One would be left to imagine how he felt during these times. The anticipation of overseas deployment must have weighed heavily on his mind. He had said his good-byes to a couple of his closest friends, in recent days, one of whom would not return home after the war. Now he faced the certainty that he was soon to be separated from home. In this letter we wrote:

> *We're going to have a physical examination on Tuesday this week. Three doctors are going to examine us - a Major, and two Captains. I guess this is the one that determines whether we'll go overseas or not. I expect that we'll be going pretty soon now, and the way I feel now, the sooner it is the better I'll like it.*
>
> *Well I'm going to close for this time, so send my best regards to your mother and father.*
>
> *I'll be seeing you.*
> *Love,*
> *Lou*

Bedford Airdrome, March 28, 1943

Fifth Air Force Insignia

"On May 9, 1943, the 348th Fighter Group moved to Camp Shanks, New York. Here is where they made their final preparations for overseas shipment. When the 348th Fighter Group boarded the Army transport ship, Henry Gibbons, on May 14, 1943, there was still some doubt among some of the personnel as to which war the group would be entering. The ship left the wharf at Weehawken, New Jersey, the next day and headed south into the Atlantic. All doubts disappeared as the transport passed through the Panama Canal enroute to the Pacific on the twenty-first of May." [5]

Destination: *"Somewhere in the Western Pacific."*

---

[5] From *Kearby's Thunderbolts* © John Stanaway, Schiffer Publ. Ltd. and used by permission of the author. (Page 17)

Chapter

★

4

This Place Called New Guinea
June 1943 - November 1944

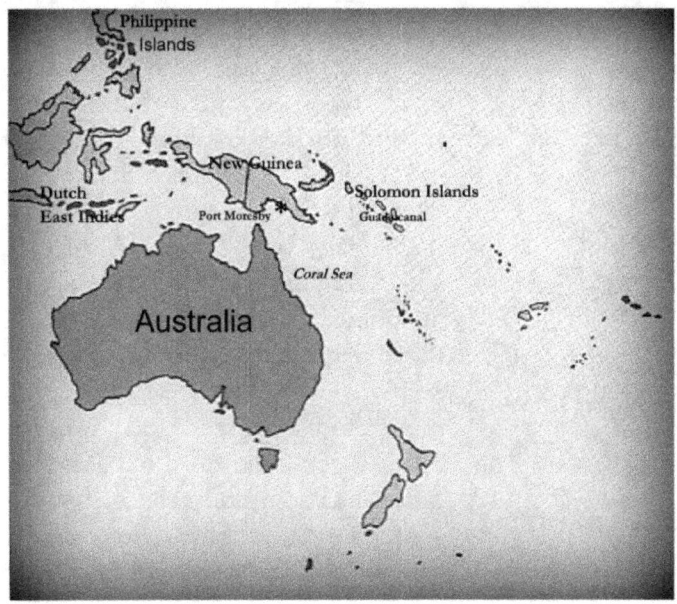

"By early June 1943, the 348th Fighter Group was making its way towards their first operational base in New Guinea. On June 4th the Henry Gibbons dropped anchor off Bora Bora in the Society Islands.

Arriving at this island was described as a beautiful and pleasant change from the pervasive seasickness on board the ship during the voyage across the Pacific. The 342nd Fighter Squadron arrived at Ward's Drome, five miles northwest of Port Moresby in New Guinea on June 23, 1943." [6]

To help the soldiers understand and adjust to New Guinea and the unique challenges of jungle life they were issued pocket guides that were published by the *Special Service Division, Army Service Forces, United States Army.*

The rainy season extended from November to March. The extreme heat and heavy rain, which resulted in hot steamy dense rain forest provided a rich environment for many types of fauna and flora. In the section on Jungle Life, there was mention of various creatures that one might encounter, including various kinds of marsupials, bats, foxes and rats. There were crocodiles, and many kinds of snakes including sea snakes which were among those that were poisonous. Most areas had a lot of ants, cockroaches, flies, mosquitoes, wasps and other insects. Special care had to be taken in getting dressed as scorpions and centipedes might sometimes hole up in shoes and clothing. One of the more unpleasant experiences were encounters with leeches. They could get through to your skin no matter what

[6] From *Kearby's Thunderbolts* © John Stanaway, Schiffer Publ. Ltd. and used by permission of the author. (Page 22)

was worn. The advise was to get rid of them as soon as possible, but to use caution as bad sores could result from tearing them off your skin.

Mosquitoes were quite plentiful and were more than just a nuisance. Some mosquitoes carried malaria, while others carried dengue fever and filariasis. Mosquito control was emphasized since the diseases they carried could incapacitate large numbers of the troops. The men were educated in preventative measures which included the use of mosquito nets over the bunks and wearing protective clothing, particularly at dusk and dawn.

> *There are plenty of mosquitoes here now, but I suppose the rain will bring more. They've got a sign up here coming into this place, and it says, "Through these portals pass the best damn mosquito bait in the world." On the other side it says, "I told you so." Boy if you only knew how true that sign is. I won't be sorry when they tell us we can leave this place.*

Port Moresby, New Guinea, September 29, 1943

(From the Sven L. Sandstrom collection)
Pocket Guide to New Guinea: Special Service Division, U.S. Army

We do have quite a time with the mosquitoes here, but we get used to them after a while. Yes, we have mosquito nets over our bunks, otherwise we wouldn't be able to sleep. The idea is to get under the net before the mosquitoes do, and sometimes that's quite a job. We have a system though, so we only get one or two in with us, then we hunt them up with a flashlight and kill them, then we can sleep peacefully.

Port Moresby, New Guinea, November 11, 1943

In addition to mosquito control, prophylactic measures against malaria included the use of drugs such as Atabrine. Rumors of Atabrine having harmful effects were dispelled in the pocket guide. The soldiers were reminded that Atabrine had been successful in preventing and curing malaria. Later in the war, information circulated about the success of those "little pills" in helping to keep the men from contracting malaria.

I can just imagine how your boss felt when his son came home on leave, after three and a half years. That's a long time to be away from home. You spoke about how yellow he looked, from taking them pills. Well most of the fellows get that way after taking them for a while. I don't think

---

August 1, 1943

U.S. Navy patrol boat, PT-109, commanded by the future U.S. President., Lt. John F. Kennedy, was rammed and sunk by the Japanese destroyer, Amagiri. After swimming for three days among the islands off the Solomons, survivors of the PT-109, including Lt. Kennedy were rescued by the U.S. Navy.

August 25, 1943

Allied troops completed the occupation of New Georgia in the Solomon Islands.

September 1943

Col. Neel Kearby, the Group Commander of the 348th Fighter Group, shot down his first enemy aircraft in Japanese stronghold near Wewak, New Guinea.

I've gotten that way, but then of course I can't tell myself. It goes away in a very short time after you stop taking them, so it's nothing to worry about. Those little pills have done an awful lot towards winning the war, as you've probably read about. They've kept a great majority of the fellows from getting malaria, and keeping them on the job.

Somewhere in the Western Pacific, May 28, 1945

Prevention of Dengue Fever, on the other hand, was limited to mosquito control. There was a higher incidence of Dengue Fever during the rainy season, with a peak incidence in January and February. In a letter sent later in the war, my dad wrote about having Dengue Fever. He wrote in response to news from my mom that her cousin had contracted some type of fever while stationed in the jungles of South America.

I'm sorry to hear your cousin Bob is so sick, and I hope he gets over it all right. I've never heard of any disease that has them effects, but that's something that you can't tell about these tropical diseases. I've been pretty fortunate so far that I haven't been sick. I had a slight touch of Dengue fever a couple of times, but I got over them all right without having to go to the hospital for it.

Somewhere in the Western Pacific, April 29, 1945

In several letters my dad wrote about the extreme heat in New Guinea. Temperatures could go up as high as 130 degrees or more and it didn't always cool off much at night. Depending on the time of year and the night-time rain, some evenings would get cooler and other times it barely went down into the 90's.

It sure is plenty hot down here. It's like summer all the time here, only it's hotter than it is back home.

It's almost time for the rainy season now, and they say it really rains too. It comes down about the same time every day, and it comes down in buckets.

Port Moresby, New Guinea, September 29, 1943

I don't imagine there's any place that's worse than here. If there is I'd like to know about it. Boy, you think it gets hot back home in the summer, but it really gets hot here. One day we looked at the thermometer, and believe it or not, it registered 130 degrees in the shade. We've had hotter days than that too. Of course we don't mind it too much though, because we're more or less used to the heat now.

Finschhafen, New Guinea, December 24, 1943

You asked if it was hot here nights, or if it cooled off. Well I'll tell you, it rains here every night (and I do mean rains), and that cools it off so we can sleep good. Some mornings when we wake up, it's so damp that we start shivering from the cold. It gets hot again as soon as the sun comes up, so then we start sweating again.

September 26, 1943

U.S. aircraft attacked Japanese airstrips at Wewak in New Guinea. More than sixty Japanese aircraft were destroyed, and six enemy ships were sunk.

October 4, 1943

U.S. Navy launched an attack on Japanese outpost on Wake Island.

October 7, 1943

The Japanese executed approximately 100 American POW's on Wake Island.

November 20, 1943

U.S. troops invaded Makin and Tarawa in the Gilbert Islands.

December 1943

The 348th Fighter Group was recognized for its success with an award of a Distinguished Unit Citation.

Life is just one great big bowl of cherries - never a dull moment.

Finschhafen, New Guinea, February 27, 1944

I'm more or less used to it [the heat] by now, but it's still too hot to suit me. It's pretty cool at night though. The temperature must go down to about 95 or 100 degrees then, and I'm not kidding when I say that either. It really gets hot around here in the daytime. It's usually up around 130 or 135 degrees. Maybe you'd better forget all about your trip to the South Seas, unless you like hot weather.

Finschhafen, New Guinea, December 27, 1943

Mosquitoes, extreme heat and red alerts were among the challenges facing the soldiers on a daily basis. The first red alert happened shortly after my dad arrived in New Guinea. The Japanese were targeting the airstrip where my dad was stationed in Port Moresby.

Speaking of air raids, we experienced our first one a short while ago, and it caused a little bit of excitement. Everybody was jumping out of the bed half asleep and running for their fox-holes (including me). We might just as well have stayed in bed though, because them near-sighted Nips couldn't hit the side of a barn door with a basketball. Oh well, it was fun while it lasted anyway.

Port Moresby, New Guinea, September 29, 1943

I go to bed every night around ten o'clock when the lights go out. We usually talk for an hour or so before going to sleep, then we get up a couple of times during the night for "red alerts," so you can see how much we sleep. You should have seen us last night. After I had finished writing your letter, it started to rain, and boy, it really came down in buckets too. Well, anyway, we were sitting here writing and talking, and all of a sudden there was a loud clap of thunder. Well I'm telling you, it sounded just like a bomb, and we just threw our stuff down and ran out of the tent. The fellow in front of me fell down going out the door and I fell over him. Then I got up and fell over one of the tent ropes, and after I got untangled from that, I finally got to the fox-hole. You would have laughed if you saw the scramble we made. The reason we fell all over ourselves, was because they put the lights out right away, and it was pitch black so we couldn't see a thing in front of us. We finally found out it was just thunder, so we went back to our writing and talking again. It gave us quite a start there at first, which is only natural, but we got over it all right. It's just as I told you, there's never a dull moment over here.

Saidor, New Guinea, March 14, 1944

There were many times when the red alerts interrupted sleep, but it was most inconvenient when they happened during a time of illness. My dad described being sick one night and getting up to take cover in the foxhole.

I'm feeling better now; I'm right in the "pink." I didn't have any jungle fever at that time; whatever gave you that idea? I just had a little fever from working out in the hot sun too long and too hard (ahem). I only had the fever one night, and I was all better again the next day, but I'm telling you, that was a miserable night, and I'm not kidding. I had a case of the "G.I.'s," better known to you as diarrhea, at the same time, and to top it off, we had two or three "red alerts" that night that I had to get up for. Some fun! Boy you can't beat this New Guinea; there's never a dull moment.

New Guinea, March 12, 1944

My dad described what they had for entertainment on the base. After long days in the hot sun, preparing planes with armaments to carry out their missions, many of the fellows would spend time either writing letters to home or watching one of the many films that had been sent from back home:

It sure was a relief in a way, not to have to put on heavy clothing now that the winter months are here, but I'd still rather be back in good old Worcester. When I get back again, it will probably take me about five years to get used to New England weather again. Yes, we have movies here where we are. They have a movie someplace around here every night, and we have all the latest ones too. About the best comedy I saw was "The More the Merrier." That was really a funny picture. We also saw Irving Berlin's, "This is the Army," and boy that was really a swell picture. You see, we don't stand short on anything over here. We get everything we need over here, (except, of course, for a little loving now and then, but I guess we can stand it all right.). We even have music with our meals over here. One of the fellows brought over a whole lot of his records with him. We have a loud-speaking system in our Mess Hall, so he plays his records for us during our meals. He's got all kinds of records too. He's got classical, semi-classical, old time, popular, cow-boy, and all kinds you can think of. His folks send him the popular ones from home too, so we keep up with all the new songs. He got a new one lately, and it's my favorite. It's "You'll Never Know," with Frank Sinatra. Boy that's really a swell song. We've even got "Pistol

Packin' Mama," and I understand that is, or should I say was number one on the Hit Parade. What's the matter are you going bomb happy or something back home picking a song like that for number one?

Port Moresby, New Guinea, November 11, 1943

In many of his letters, my dad would talk about the latest movies that were sent for the men in his group. He answered an inquiry from my mom about where they watched the movies:

You asked if we have our movies inside or outside. Well we have them outside and if you saw us sometimes, you'd probably think that we were whacky or something. Some nights it's raining cats and dogs, and I mean it really rains over here too, but still we sit out there and watch the show anyway. We have our raincoats on, but still we usually get soaked, and then we have to change our clothes when we get back to the tent again. We have the movie projector under cover, so that's why the show can continue whether it rains or not. The only thing that will stop the show is a "Red Alert," and in a case like that, we just dive into our fox-holes and start praying. A "Red Alert" means that there are enemy planes about five to ten minutes flying time away.

Finschhafen, New Guinea, December 28, 1943

My dad wrote about a magazine clipping he received from my mom. He continued with how the members of his squadron responded when the Japanese would bomb the area where they were stationed .

As far as the picture of the Jap on the other side of the clipping, I'll probably be able to kick him for you. Where we are now, we can watch our planes bombing and strafing the Japs. Some fun!! It isn't so much fun though when they come over to bomb us. We don't mind it so much though, because we're more or less used to it. But we still sweat them out when we get the "alerts." When we hear the bombs falling, we dive into our fox-holes, but they haven't hit too close to us yet.

Finschhafen, New Guinea, February 16, 1944

In some of his letters, my dad gave updates on how his Squadron was doing in terms of numbers of Japanese planes shot down. Because of censorship, there was certain information he couldn't share, but sometimes he could give a general idea of the area where they were located.

You're not kidding, our group is doing wonders over here. We've got 178 [Japanese planes] to our credit now, with only two of ours shot down. We might get a citation for having the world's record, and when and if we get 200 planes to our credit, we'll get a citation for that too. Yes, we're in New Guinea, but I'm not bragging about it. We don't see any action, but we can watch our planes bombing and strafing the Japs a short distance away. We can also hear the field artillery guns going off all the time, and see the destroyers up the coast shelling the Japs. We've had a few bombing raids, but I don't know if you would call that action or not. You might though, if you saw how fast we move for our fox-holes when we hear the bombs falling. They all sound as though they're going to land right on top of us, so it gives us a kind of funny feeling, if you know what I mean. You asked if we were near the front where we are now. Well, this is the most advanced fighter base on the island, so you can draw your own conclusion on that. I'll give you three guesses , and the first two won't count. You'll find the 348th Group right on the ball at all times.

Finschhafen, New Guinea, February 23, 1944

In some of his letters, my dad would write about some of the opinions that had circulated about the South Sea Islands. Like many civilians, my mom had an idea that the islands were beautiful, with coral reefs, coconut palms, green jungles, and native women dressed in sarongs. My dad painted a different picture based on his experience in New Guinea.

> *So you envy me being in a warm place do you? Well I'll trade places with you any day. I like warm weather, but I don't like hot weather. Yes, I know how you hate to freeze, Ginny, but I think if you came over here for a while you'd agree with me that cold weather is a whole lot better than this. As for your going to the South Seas, I imagine some of the places are nice, the way they advertize them, but take my advice and don't come anywhere near New Guinea.*

Finschhafen, New Guinea, December 26, 1943

> *You want to know how the girls are over here? Well, they're all pretty dark complected, and we don't see them unless we go up to the native villages. They don't wear sarongs like Dorothy Lamour, but they do wear grass skirts. A few of them wear something similar to a sarong, but not many.*

Port Moresby, New Guinea, November 11, 1943

The native customs and life styles were very different from anything the American soldiers had experienced. The native islanders were not savages, cannibals and head hunters as some might have thought when they came to New Guinea, the Bismarcks and the Solomons. Some of the natives may have looked wild, as they held on to their primitive costume and culture, but they were pretty civilized and sophisticated. My dad wrote about one strange custom he witnessed while stationed in New Guinea:

I saw a funny thing the other day. We were riding down the road and we saw a whole line of natives walking along. There were about five men, twenty women, and about five children. The men were walking along leisurely, and the women and kids all had big heavy bundles on their backs, and they were just staggering along. When the natives want to get married here, they buy their wives from the parents for three pounds, which is worth about $9.60. If they don't have any money, they give them three pigs instead. Boy, what a system! I think I'll try that sometime, and see if I have any luck.

Finschhafen, New Guinea, December 28, 1943

(From the Sven L. Sandstrom collection)
Natives in New Guinea

He later responded to remarks my mom made about this native custom:

Well, I'm glad that you agree with me that $9.60 or three pigs is pretty cheap for a wife. I think it's a good idea. I'll have to try it out when I get home, *and see if it works. No, none of the fellows have considered buying one yet, but maybe if we stay here much longer they will. Notice I said 'they,' and not 'we.' I don't think I'll ever go as far as that. I've got a little sense anyway, (I think).*

Finschhafen, New Guinea, February 28, 1944

When the troops were first being oriented to the islands, they were told that it was very important to get along well with the native people. The natives were just as anxious as the Allies to see the Japanese thrown off the islands. Their homes and gardens had been bombed and destroyed, and their family members had been tortured and killed. In many instances the local inhabitants had helped the Allied troops as guides, carriers, and stretcher bearers, or had cared for soldiers who were temporarily separated from their bases.

"On August 18, 1943, there was one such instance where the natives aided a pilot from the 342nd Fighter Squadron. Sixteen P-47's, escorting transports to Wau, were flying in formation when they went into the overcast. Two of the planes did not emerge. The pilot of one of the planes bailed out and when his parachute opened, it became tangled in the treetops, leaving him dangling over the ground where he was a target for Japanese patrols. He cut himself loose, but when he plunged through the branches to the jungle floor, he fractured his leg. It would be three days and two nights crawling on the jungle ground before he was found by some friendly natives. They splinted his leg and carried him back to their village. They cared for him until local troops came along and eventually he was returned to his base at Port Moresby. The other pilot, Flight Officer Wilfrid Desilets was not found." [7]

Over fifty years later, the body of F/O Wilfrid Desilets, a native of Worcester, Massachusetts, was found in the cock pit of his downed P-47 in the jungles of New Guinea. His remains were eventually returned to his surviving family to be buried in Worcester.

---

[7] From *Kearby's Thunderbolts* © John Stanaway, Schiffer Publ. Ltd. and used by permission of the author. (Page 32 - 33)

There were plenty of stories of life on the islands which circulated among the troops, and my dad wrote of one such story he heard shortly after arriving overseas in 1943. This came in a letter that was written later in the war:

I heard this one shortly after I came overseas. It seems that during your first month over here, if there's a fly in your coffee cup, you throw away the coffee and get a fresh cup. During your second month, when the same thing happens, you just pick the fly out with your spoon and throw it away. During your third month, you just blow the fly to the other side of the cup, and drink the coffee that way. Then after your fourth month, you throw away the coffee and eat the fly - because it's fresh meat!! Of course, it isn't quite that bad, but it gives you an idea of the kind of stories they dream up. What a sense of humor.

Somewhere in the Western Pacific, May 30, 1945

(From the Sven L. Sandstrom collection)

February 23, 1944

U.S.   Forces bombarded   the Mariana   Islands, which   included Saipan, Tinian, and Guam.   This strategic point would give   the   U.S.   the bases from which to launch   bombing strikes   against mainland Japan.

March 1944

Col.   Neel Kearby, Commander   of   the 348th Fighter Group was killed during aerial combat in New Guinea.   He   was awarded   the posthumous Congressional Medal of Honor.

April - May 1944

The Allies invaded Hollandia in New Guinea   in   April and a month later Biak Island.

In a V-mail dated January 26, 1944, my dad apologized for not writing sooner:

I'm sorry I haven't written for the past few days but we've been trying to modernize our tent here.

At a later date he went on to describe modernizing the tent and living quarters in New Guinea.

You asked what we do when we modernize out tents. Well, we just put floors in them, build a rail around it, put up shelves, build tables and chairs, and things like that. We've only had floors in the last two areas we've been in. Before that, we just put our tents and bunks on the ground. We have to have floors here though, because the ground gets awfully damp after it rains. It rains almost every night in the rainy season, and I'm telling you, it really comes down in buckets too. In the dry season, it's just the opposite. We don't have any rain at all then. It goes from one extreme to the other.

Saidor, New Guinea, March 19, 1944

Have you ever missed one of your neckerchiefs? Well if you have, I'm the one that's got it. I remember you told me to hold it for you one night when we went to the show, so

I put it in my pocket and never returned it to you again. I've got it over here with me now. It brings back some very pleasant memories. I keep it on the shelf aside of my bed, with your picture. Yes, I've got your picture here too, the colored one you sent me when I was in Colorado. Remember? I've also got all the snapshots you sent me, and I've got them in my album.

Finschhafen, New Guinea, February 28, 1944

I've got that little colored picture that you sent to me when I was at Lowry Field right next to my bunk, so that's the last thing I see before going to bed. By having that there, I have pleasant dreams.

Boy, are you lazy, writing your letters in bed! What am I talking about? I'm doing the same thing. In fact, I write most of my letters in bed. Of course, you know, it isn't that I'm lazy or anything, it's just that it's more comfortable.

Saidor, New Guinea, March 29, 1944

Sometimes, despite the complaining of the extreme heat and living conditions in New Guinea, my dad would make a comment on the moonlight and beautiful sunsets:

Boy, I've got so much mail to answer now that I don't know where to start. I've got 38 letters to answer so I guess I'll be kept pretty busy for a while. I'll probably have writer's cramp by the time I'm through. I could use a good secretary, so how about coming down here to help me out? Just think if you came down here to help me, I could show you around these beautiful (?) South Sea Islands. The only time I think it's nice here, is on a moonlit night, but I can't enjoy it without a girl. It really is beautiful though, when there's a full moon. (a lot of good it's doing me.)

Finschhafen, New Guinea, February 29, 1944

You ought to see the beautiful full moon we've got tonight. You should be here to help me enjoy it, then everything would be complete.

Finschhafen, New Guinea, March 8, 1944

(From the Sven L. Sandstrom collection)
Sunset in New Guinea

Letters from home kept my dad connected with what was going on with his family and friends. He not only heard about what was going on back in good old Worcester, but he was kept informed about his buddies and where they were in their training and preparations for overseas deployment.

I understand that Gus finally got his papers through, so he's going to Cadet School now. I hope he makes out all right. I suppose you know that Russell is a Sergeant now, and he got his wings for

Aerial Gunner. I sure was happy when I heard that. I've been sorry ever since I left the States that I didn't go for that too. The reason I'd like to be a Gunner is that they see plenty of action. Well, I guess I'll have to be satisfied being just a plain Armorer, and let it go at that. I hear that Russell is, or should I say was, home on furlough. Did you see him any?

Port Moresby, New Guinea, September 29, 1943

I hear that Russell got married when he was home on his furlough. Boy was I surprised when I heard that. He wrote to me and said that he was thinking about getting married if he got a furlough, but I didn't think that he would. I knew he would eventually, but I thought he'd wait until after the war was over. Well, more power to him and I wish them both a lot of luck and happiness.

Port Moresby, New Guinea, October 5, 1943

(From the Sven L. Sandstrom collection)
P-47, somewhere in New Guinea

My dad expressed how he missed home in many of his letters. Birthdays and holidays were challenging in many ways. His first Christmas overseas was void of the usual Christmas spirit, but filled with the hope that he would be home the following year. However, it wouldn't be until 1945, that he would celebrate the holidays in good old Worcester, Massachusetts again. He missed his family and friends, but stayed in contact through letter writing.

I'm writing now to wish you a Very Happy Birthday. I hope this letter gets there in time for it. I can't get even so much as a card over here to send to you, so I sent my mother some money to get you something. I don't know what it will be, but I hope you like it anyway. Well how is everything going in Worcester now-a-days? I suppose practically all of the fellows are in the Service by now aren't they? I heard from Russell and Danny when they were home on furlough, and they said it was kind of quiet around there.

Port Moresby, New Guinea, October 28, 1943

Well, I suppose you're beginning to think I've forgotten all about you, because I haven't written for so long now. I'm really very sorry about it though, but we've just moved to a new camp area, and we've been working day and night to get it all set up. We've got it pretty well finished now though, so I'll be able to catch up on my mail.

Right now I've got five letters and a Christmas card from you to answer, and also a Christmas card from your mother and father. In all, I've got forty-one letters to answer, so you can see I haven't been doing any writing lately. I'll have writer's cramp by the time I get through answering them all.

Boy I'd like to have seen you at that party dressed

up as a gun moll. I probably would have fallen through the floor too if I saw you like that. After all, I've always known you to be dressed up nice and neat all the time. Don't tell me there weren't any fellows at all at that party? Gee whiz, what did you do all night? I never heard of a Halloween party without both fellows and girls. Remember that Halloween party we went to two years ago? I think that was my first date with you, wasn't it?

Well how does Worcester look now with all the lights on again? I bet it looks good. I've forgotten what it looks like, because when I was going home from Westover Field and Bedford, everything was all dimmed out. You're not kidding boy, I sure hope that means that the end of the war isn't too far away, because I sure will be glad to get back home again. This is the longest I've ever been away from home at one time.

By the way, we've set a new world record in our Group now. We've shot down 101 enemy planes, and we've only lost one. Our Squadron has 39 of them, and we're ahead of all the others. Our former Group Commander has got seventeen planes to his credit now. What do you think of that record that we've got? Pretty good, eh?

Finschhafen, New Guinea, December 23, 1943

I heard about Russell being home on another ten day furlough, and I sure was glad to hear it. The last I heard, he was up in Maine someplace. He said that he expects to go to England. At least he'll be in a whole lot better place than I am.

As far as the birthday present I sent to you, I'm glad that you liked it. I'd like to have done more, but gee whiz, I can't get anything at all over here. When I want to get anything for anybody, I have to send the money to my mother and she has to get it for me. I sure hope things will get back to normal again soon. Of course, I shouldn't kick, because there are fellows that have been overseas longer than me, and they're a whole lot worse off than I am. I've only been here for six months now, but it's still too long for me. Yesterday marked our sixth month over here. We landed on June 23. Boy, I'm a regular old veteran.

Well anyway, to get back to that bracelet again, it sure looks as though it's nice by the drawing you made of it. I'll have to go over to see it when I get home again, and of course, to see you too. I don't know when that will be, but I hope the time isn't too far away.

Yes, we have a radio to listen to over here. We get re-broadcasts of a lot of the programs, like Bob Hope, Hit Parade, Kraft Music Hall, etc., but I haven't listened to it for quite a while now. I'm usually too busy at night, writing letters, to bother with that.

Well here it is Christmas Eve tonight, but boy, it doesn't seem like it to me. Gee whiz, no snow or anything. I guess I'll have to be satisfied and dream of a White Christmas this year. This is the first time I've ever been away from home for Christmas.

Our Chaplain is going to have Christmas Carol singing tonight, and then tomorrow, he's going to have a Christmas Service. Well at least that will be nice anyway.

Finschhafen, New Guinea, December 24, 1943

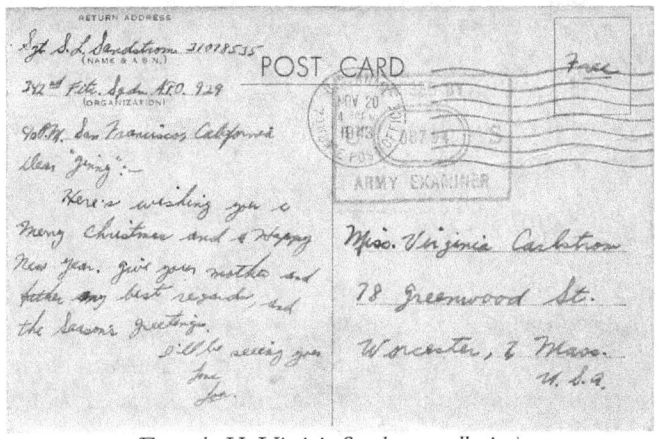

(From the H. Virginia Sandstrom collection)

There wasn't much Christmas spirit in me this year either, but I tried to make the best of everything under these circumstances. I sure hope we're together again next Christmas, and who knows, maybe we will be. Might as well be an optimist anyway, rather than a pessimist.

Finschhafen, New Guinea, January 10, 1944

(From the Sven L. Sandstrom collection)
My dad at the armament tent Somewhere in the Western Pacific.

Dear "Ginny," -

Hello again, here I am with another excuse. I haven't written to you for a few days, so I hope you'll forgive me. I suppose you're getting sick of all these excuses, but that's how it goes. I haven't had any Air Mail envelopes, or stamps, so I haven't been doing any writing. I hate to send my letters "Free" from over here, because it takes them too long to get there. A friend of mine gave me a few stamps, so they should last me a couple of days anyway.

Well anyway, I'm awfully sorry to hear about all the tough luck you had over the Christmas holidays, and I sure hope that everything is all right now again. I hope your brother pulls through everything all right. I've heard from home that just about everybody has had the flu or grippe or something this winter. I guess all you "Swedes" back home are weakening and can't take the cold weather anymore! Now if I were there, I could keep you warm (maybe) and you wouldn't have to worry about catching colds.

I'd like to go right back home now very much, because I'm sick of this damn war.

Well Ginny, I guess it's time I close for this time, but I'll write again tomorrow night. I hope this letter finds you all in the best of health.

Finschhafen, New Guinea, February 27, 1944

I just received your Valentine today, "Ginny," and I want to thank you very much for it. I'm sorry I couldn't send you a card from here, but after all, we don't have any "ten cent stores" around here. Maybe next year things will be better though, I hope.

Boy, you're not kidding, our Squadron has got a good record of knocking off Jap planes. We don't stand short you know. We've also got the best maintenance and health records too. What do you mean we can't praise the Squadron high enough? Gee whiz, do you want us to get big heads? It's only natural though, that we're proud of our outfit, and we hope to keep up the good work too. With the help of God, we'll do it.

I don't blame your brother for being glad that he'll be home again, because I'd feel the same way. I'm telling you, it's going to be a happy day when I get home again. I'm going to go out and paint

Worcester "red," and I'm not kidding. I might need some help too, so how about reserving a date for me?

Gee whiz, you said that you were going to close your letter for that time, before you got warmed up. You don't want to let that worry you, because I don't mind getting long letters. In fact, the longer they are, the better I like them. The only trouble is I can't write long letters in return, but I can try anyway.

Finschhafen, New Guinea, March 2, 1944

I got a letter from Russell today, and boy was I glad to hear from him. It's the first I've heard from him since he went overseas. As you probably know, he's in England now and he is also a S/Sgt. He said he likes it over there, but of course he misses home, and especially Gurlie. Well, with the help of God we'll all be back home together again, and I sure hope it's soon.

Finschhafen, New Guinea, March 8, 1944

My dad wrote about waiting to get a furlough, and as he was writing he heard one of his favorite Glenn Miller songs:

Yes, I'm supposed to get a furlough, but I haven't gotten it yet. I guess I'll just have to wait my turn, because they can't send everybody at once. You're not kidding, it's going to be a nice change for me. It's going to feel good to see some civilization for a change. After all I haven't seen any since I got here, which was last June 23rd. If you think that isn't a long time to stay in a place like this, you want to try it some time. Pardon me, but they're playing

"Moonlight Serenade" on the phonograph now with Glenn Miller's orchestra, and I've got to listen to it. Boy, what a swell song. I'd like to be dancing to it right now with you. Well to get back to my furlough, I don't know if I'll fly there or not, but I think so. I'll fly part of the way anyway. When I get down there [Australia], I'll get something for you and send it to you.

I haven't seen any Jap prisoners here, but some of the fellows have, and they say that they are awfully small in comparison to us Yanks. A few of them speak English, and they seem to think they're on some island off the California coast, so you can see what kind of propaganda Tojo tells them.

Finschhafen, New Guinea, March 14, 1944

Hideki Tojo, a general of the Imperial Japanese Army, was Prime Minister of Japan during WWII, and responsible for the Japanese attack on Pearl Harbor. His caricature was often used in anti-Japanese propaganda art during the war. Just before his arrest at the end of the war, Tojo attempted suicide by shooting himself in the chest. He survived and was brought to trial for war crimes. Tojo was found guilty of being a war criminal and was executed by hanging on December 23, 1948.

Guess what? I finally got my camera today, and boy was I glad to get it. I'll send you some pictures as soon as I can, but don't expect them too soon though, because we haven't got our Photo Lab built up here yet. I'm enclosing one picture that a fellow took of me a few weeks ago. I just got it today. It's a lousy picture, but I warned you that it would be. The printing on the sign says, "342nd Fighter Squadron - First Thunderbolt Squadron in the S.W. Pacific" Well at least the sign is pretty anyway.

New Guinea, March 26, 1944

(From the Sven L. Sandstrom collection)
My dad standing next to Squadron sign:
342nd Fighter Squadron.
First Thunderbolt Squadron in the SW Pacific.

What do you mean when you say we men are all alike? I just asked how you could have fun without any fellows at your party. I didn't think it was possible, but maybe I was wrong. I don't know. I'd like to go to a party with all girls too, and boy, could I have some fun!! oops! What am I saying? Anyway, when I see a female again, I'll probably stand and stare at it, and wonder what it is. (or something).

Finschhafen, New Guinea, February 23, 1944

(From the Sven L. Sandstrom collection)
My dad, April 1944, Saidor New Guinea

O.K. Ginny, I'll give up. I won't argue with you any more about how you girls can have any fun at parties without fellows. It isn't that I agree with you on it, you understand, it's just that I know I couldn't win the argument anyway. I still don't see how you can do it though. As for these "Stag Parties" that the fellows have, - well that's different. Now you shouldn't go talking about those poor 4-F's like that, although I will admit that there are a lot of them that think they're in demand because of the man-shortage. I bet they get plenty of dates though! Think of all the fun I could have if I was back there now. At least I'd have my uniform to help me get some dates anyway! Oh well, the war can't last forever, and then we'll all be home again soon. Then we'll see who rates. Maybe a lot of us will be 4-F's after we get out of this d--- place, so what's the difference anyway.

Yes I'm going to go to Australia on my furlough, but I don't know when. It should be soon though. At least within the next 99 years or so. Well I can't tell you where I'll be leaving from (military secret you know), but you were right in your supposition. I still don't think you can figure out where I am though. Tell me where you think I am, so I can see how close to right you are. I'll be able to tell you these things about where I've been and what I've seen, etc., etc., after the war is over. Until then though, we have censorship regulations to comply with.

Saidor, New Guinea, April 4, 1944

(From the Sven L. Sandstrom collection)
P-47's flying in formation.

Hello again, and how is everything in Worcester these days?. You said that you're not used to the night life any more. Well, I guess we'll have to get you on the beam again, after I get back to Worcester.

You asked if there was any such thing as a B-25 Mitchell. Gee whiz, don't tell me you don't know your country's aircraft? Well I'll tell you, the B-25 is a medium bomber, made by the North American Aircraft Company, and is commonly referred to as the "Billy Mitchell." It is a twin engine plane, and it also has a twin rudder. They are very good for low altitude bombing and strafing. Does that answer your question? Anything else you want to know, just ask me. (ahem)

Saidor, New Guinea, April 16, 1944

(From the Sven L. Sandstrom collection)
My dad, Cpl. Charles Kenny, and Cpl. Don MacAuley
Saidor, New Guinea, April 1944

My mother told me in one of her letters that you sent over a card and a beautiful spray of flowers when my grandmother died. Thanks very much for sending them, Ginny. I thought it was darn swell of you to do that.

I wasn't surprised when you said that you came home with some stockings and an ivy plant, when you started out to get a dress and a hat. I guess I know you well enough to expect that. If I remember correctly, you've done that a few times before too, and told me about it. Oh well, that's just like a woman anyway. You never find us men doing that when we go shopping, (ahem). We just go up and get whatever we want, and go back home again. You ought to try it sometime. It's really very simple.

I haven't had any of my snapshots developed yet, but I'll get around to it someday. You see, our photography men are working on a scrapbook for the Squadron, and they're not going to develop any more of our films until they get it finished. Did my mother ever show you the scrapbook that I sent home from the states? If she didn't, ask her to show you sometime. Well anyway, this one is going to be similar to that, only it's going to be bigger and better, and it's going to deal with the 342nd overseas. I think I'll send my films to Australia to get developed while I'm waiting for them to finish the scrapbook. It will take about a month to get them back, so I'm afraid you'll have to wait a little longer before getting any of my pictures. You're not missing much anyway, so just have a little patience.

Saidor, New Guinea, April 19, 1944

I'm sorry I haven't written for quite a while, but I haven't been able to, because we've been busy over here. I haven't written any letters at all now for about two weeks, in fact we haven't had any mail for quite a while now either. I won't be able to write very much for the next week or two, but after that I'll be writing regularly again.

Yesterday marked our first year overseas although in a way it doesn't seem that long. Other times though, it seems as though it's been longer than that. I hope I'm back in the States before another year is up.

V-mail written from
Wakde, New Guinea, May 16, 1944

(From the Sven L. Sandstrom collection)
The squadron's pet monkey, "Nancy"
Somewhere in New Guinea

Dear "Ginny." -

Well, I'm finally getting around to writing again. I'm sorry I haven't written sooner, but we've moved again, and we haven't been able to do any writing, because we've been pretty busy. You'll notice that we're still using the old A.P.O. number though. We finally received some mail, and I've got five of your letters to answer now.

I got a letter from Signe Anderson yesterday, that was written on April 24th, and she said that neither they nor Gurlie had heard from Russell for a week. I sure hope that he's all right and nothing has

June 15, 1944

The U.S. began the invasion of the Mariana Islands, landing troops on Saipan. The Marines were met by an enemy that was ready to fight to the death. The Japanese made their last and largest suicidal "Banzai" attack of World War II. Referred to as "devils from hell," the Japanese soldiers would charge the enemy en masse without regard to the number of casualties, even their own death.

June 19, 1944

U.S. carrier based fighters shot down more than 200 Japanese aircraft in what would later be called the "Marianas Turkey Shoot."

happened to him. The last I heard, he had twenty missions over Germany to his credit, and he was on a leave in Scotland. Maybe he moved and didn't have time to write, at least I hope so anyway. Well, I guess I'll have to wait and see, and hope for the best.

Well I guess I'll close for this time, hoping to hear from you again soon. Send my best regards to your mother and father.

I'll be seeing you
Love, Lou

P.S. Thank you for the stick of gum you sent in this letter. It was delicious.

Wakde, New Guinea, May 28, 1944

(From the Sven L. Sandstrom collection)
Wakde Island

When I told you about the "red alerts," I mean that that means they're about five minutes flying time away from us. They don't actually come over and bomb us every time we have a "red alert," but most of the time they do. We never know if they're coming over or not, so we get out of bed anyway, just in case they do, so we can get into our fox-holes in a hurry.

Wakde, New Guinea, May 29, 1944

In early June, 1944, all eyes were on the coast of France in the region of Normandy. In one of the largest amphibious invasions in history, approximately 156,000 American, British and Canadian troops landed on five beaches, codenamed Gold, Juno, Sword, Utah and Omaha, along a fifty mile stretch of France. British and Canadian forces took Gold, Juno and Sword with little opposition. The Americans faced some opposition at Utah Beach and the casualties were fairly light. Omaha Beach was the most heavily fortified and Americans faced fierce opposition. There were over 2,000 American casualties at Omaha Beach, most of which came in the first few hours of the invasion. Operation Overlord, which began on D-Day, June 6, 1944, lasted until Allied forces crossed the River Seine on August 19, 1944 and France was liberated from Nazi Germany's control. The Normandy invasion was a major turning point and the beginning of the end of the war in Europe.

Some of the letters my dad sent home were written over a couple of days. The following letter began and was headed with June 6th. The invasion of France began on June 6th and this excerpt was probably written on the 7th since he was on the other side of the international date line. This was his immediate response to the news from Normandy as it was happening:

I was just listening to the radio a short while ago, and I heard that they've started the invasion of France now. Boy were we happy to hear that. I only hope and pray now that everything will go along well for us over there so we can end the war soon. I guess about all we can do is wait and see. I'm pretty confident though.

Wakde, New Guinea, June 6, 1944

You asked me when I thought the war would be over. Well I'll tell you, that's a pretty hard question to answer.

All I can say is that I sure hope it's soon. Well, they've finally opened the "second front" in Europe, and they're going along pretty well over in Italy now, and we're not doing so bad over here, so I guess it can't last too much longer. As someone said, "it's all over now but the fighting." Well with God's help we'll win the war soon, and we'll all be home again. By the way, today marks my second year in the Army, as you probably know.

I guess Harry expects to be going overseas now pretty soon. I got a letter from him, and he said that he made out his "last will" and "power of attorney," etc., and he's having his overseas physical exam now. Well I sure wish him a lot of luck, wherever he goes. I got a letter from my mother today, dated May 18, and she said that Gussie was supposed to be graduating from cadet school that day. I sure was glad to hear that. I guess he must be a 2nd Lieutenant now. In his last letter to me, he had said that he was soloing, so I was expecting him to graduate and get his "wings" soon. I can just imagine how happy he must feel about that, because I know how much he likes flying.

You asked if I was on the east coast of New Guinea, somewhere near Truk. I don't know where you ever got any ideas like that, but I think you'd better get a map and look at it, and you'll see where these places are. Gee whiz, Truk is above New Guinea, in fact it's even above New Britain. You said that you had it figured out that I was near either Buna or Truk. Well you're wrong in both cases. Guess again. I doubt if you can figure out where I am though, so I guess you'll have to wait until I get home, and I'll be able to tell you where I've been.

Wakde, New Guinea, June 17, 1944

(From the Sven L. Sandstrom collection)
My dad in front of downed Japanese aircraft. Wakde Island, June 1944

(From the Sven L. Sandstrom collection)
A downed Japanese aircraft, Wakde Island, June 1944

Well, Ginny, I got some bad news last night. I wrote a letter to Russell on March 15th, and I got it back again last night. On the envelope it said that he was "missing." Well you can imagine how I felt about that when I saw it. He's the best friend that I've got, and then when I see that - well I just can't believe that anything has happened to him. I don't know if it's been in the papers or anything back home, but nobody has written and told me anything about it. There's still a chance that he's all right, when he's listed as "missing," and I hope and pray that he is. I can just imagine how his folks and Gurlie feel. I wrote them both V-Mail letters last night, but I couldn't think of a thing to say or anything as to how I feel. Well I'm going to keep my hopes up, and pray that he's all right.

I was surprised when you said that you had sent me a box of candy. I hope it isn't all squashed by the time it gets here. It usually takes about two months for a package to get here, so I'll probably get it around August sometime. I'll let you know as soon as I get it though.

Wakde, New Guinea,
June 25, 1944

I haven't heard from either Russell, Harry, or Gus recently. The last I heard from them, Harry was in Munroe, Louisiana, and he was expecting to go overseas because he had his overseas physical, and made out his last will and testament and power of attorney, etc. He was supposed to be home on furlough last month, but my mother told me that he couldn't get it, so I don't know if he's left the States or not.

The last I heard from Gus, he was just starting to solo, but I forgot exactly where he was. Since then though, my mother told me that he has graduated now, and he has his "wings."

Then of course, I believe I told you about Russell in one of my letters. I wrote him a letter, and I got it back again, and on the envelope it said that he was "missing." I still haven't heard from anybody at home saying anything about it, so I don't know what the story is. I've written to just about everybody back there asking about it, but I haven't received any answer as yet. I wish they'd hurry up and write and let me know if he's all right or not. I just can't believe that anything has happened to him and I hope and pray that he's all right. You know, when you don't hear anything at all about it, it gets on your nerves, more than if you knew for a fact what the score was. Well I hope to hear from all three of them soon.

Yes, I'm thinking of taking up Air Conditioning after I get home again. You said that you don't know very much about it. Well neither do I, but it sounds interesting and I believe there's a good future in it, because it's one of the coming things. If I don't like that, I'll try diesel engines or refrigeration, or something.

Wakde, New Guinea, July, 17, 1944

Dear "Ginny" -

I just received a letter from you today, dated July 8th, and I sure was glad to hear from you again. It's the first I've heard from you for quite a while now. I'm glad to hear that you're feeling well. I'm feeling fine and in the best of health.

I haven't got time to answer it now though because I'm leaving on furlough tomorrow morning. I've got to write a couple of V-Mail letters, and then I've got to get my stuff ready. I'll probably be able to write when I get down there, so I'll write to you as soon as I get down there. I don't know how long it will take to get down there, but it will be a few days anyway.

Wakde, New Guinea, July, 27, 1944

(From the Sven L. Sandstrom collection)
My dad hanging clothes in the laundry area at his camp, Somewhere in the Western Pacific

98

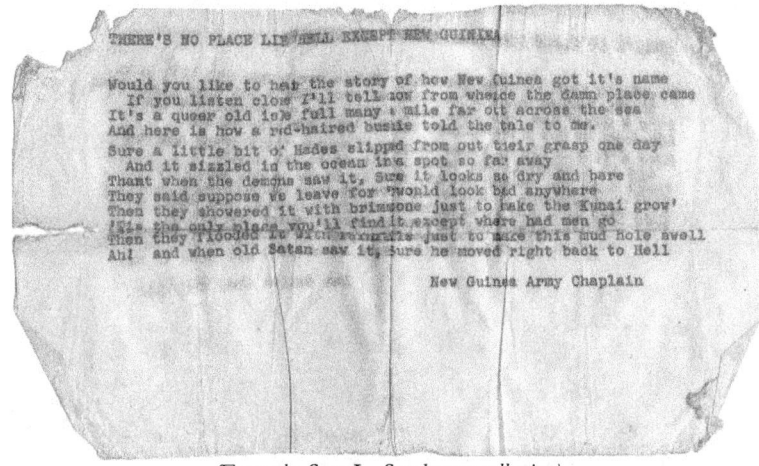

(From the Sven L. Sandstrom collection)
This was found among my dad's letters and pictures. The author is unknown.

There's No Place Like Hell Except New Guinea

Would you like to hear the story of how New Guinea got it's name
If you listen close I'll tell now from whence the damn place came
It's a queer old isle full many a mile far out across the sea
And here is how a red-haired bushie told the tale to me.
Sure a little bit of Hades slipped from out their grasp one day
And it sizzled in the ocean in a spot so far away.
That when the demons saw it, sure it looks so dry and bare
They said suppose we leave for 'twould look bad anywhere
Then they showered it with brimstone just to make the Kunai grow
'Tis the only place you'll find it except where bad men go
Then they flooded it with rainfalls just to make this mud hole swell
Ah! and when old Satan saw it, sure he moved right back to Hell.
New Guinea Army Chaplain

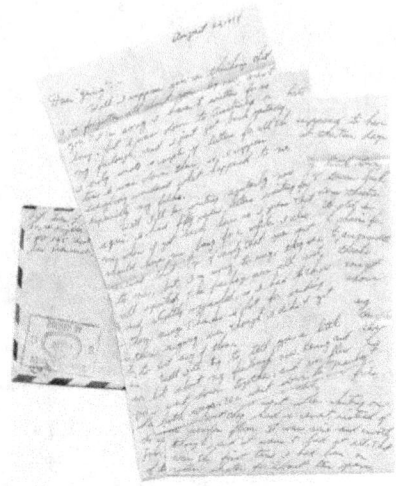

Dear "Ginny" -

Well I suppose you're thinking that I've forgotten all about you by now, aren't you? I'm sorry I haven't written for so long, but I was down to Australia on my furlough, and just got back yesterday. I only wrote a couple of letters for all the time I was down there, so I suppose everybody wondered what happened to me, especially my folks.

Well I'll be writing regularly now again. I had fifty-seven letters waiting for me when I got back here, so I guess that should keep me busy for a while. I also received that box of candy that you sent to me, but I'm sorry to say, that they were all spoiled. The package was all wet and slightly squashed, so I had to throw them away. Thanks a lot for sending them anyway, even though I didn't get to eat any of them. Well I'll try to tell you a little bit about my furlough now. Kenny and I went down together, and we flew both ways. We went down to Mackay, Australia, and we were supposed to have ten days there, but we got thirteen days out of it.

Mackay is a pretty nice little town, similar to any of our small towns back home. They only had one

modern theater there, and the others were quite old.
In the old theater, they had beach chairs for seats,
only they're big enough to accommodate two people
instead of one. Each theater has only one show a
day, and none at all on Sundays. They have their
shows at 7:45 at night.

The Red Cross had a dance every night except
Sunday for the soldiers. On Sunday nights they put
on a stage show and a movie. Every day they had
something doing for the servicemen like horseback
riding, picnics, softball, golf, steak fries, and
everything else imaginable.

Kenny and I went roller-skating one night, but they
had a cement, instead of wooden floor. It was nice
and smooth though, and it wasn't bad at all. That
was the first time I had been on roller skates for
about ten years, but much to my surprise, I didn't
fall down any.

We didn't stay at Mackay for our whole furlough
though. We went out to Sarina, which is about
twenty-five miles away from there. Boy, what a one-
horse town that is. They only had one theater out
there, and they only had a show on three nights a
week.

They had a dance two nights a week, on Thursdays
and Saturdays. All they used was a piano for the
music. On Saturday night, it was a special occasion
though, because all the farmers came into town, so
they used a drum and the piano.

If they were dancing a waltz, they'd take any song
that came into their mind, and play it in waltz time.
The same for polkas, fox-trots, and their own special
dances. For instance, they played "Home on the
Range" in waltz time once, and "Stage Door

Canteen" in polka tempo once. Some fun! I tried dancing a couple of times, but I didn't do so good, so I gave it up as a bad job. I enjoyed myself watching them do some of their own dances.

We went horseback riding while we were out there, and I was kind of stiff for a couple of days afterwards. It was a lot of fun though. We had the horses galloping all of the time, but still, I think I was more tired than the horse when we got back.

All in all, we had a pretty good time down there. One thing though, they're at least fifty years behind times from our standard of living back in the States. It was nice to get down there and away from New Guinea for a while though.

Well, I guess I'll close for this time, hoping to hear from you again soon. I've got four of your letters to answer now. Send my best regards to your mother and father.

I'll be seeing you
Love,
Lou

Wakde, New Guinea, August 22, 1944

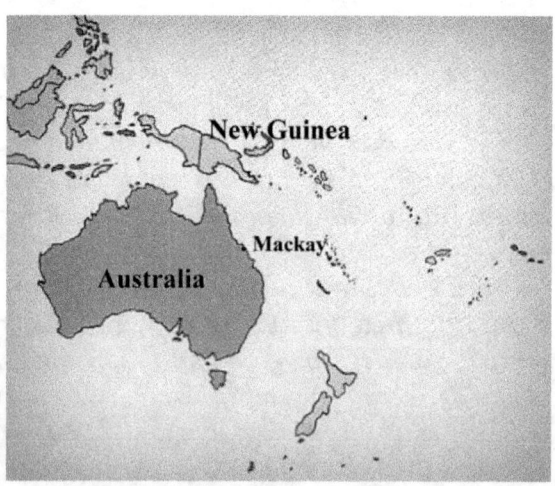

(From the Sven L. Sandstrom collection)
Pictures taken in Australia while my dad was on furlough in August 1944.

Photo courtesy of the Lawrence J. Hickey Collection
The International Historical Research Associates.
Bob Hope and Frances Langford, USO Camp Show

On February 4, 1941, the United Service Organization, (USO) was incorporated in New York. It grew out of the pooled resources of six private organizations; the Young Men's Christian Association

(YMCA), the Young Women's Christian Association (YWCA), National Catholic Community Service, National Jewish Welfare Board, Traveler's Aid Association and the Salvation Army. President Roosevelt, who appealed to these organizations to develop services for the emotional support of the troops, became the first USO Honorary Chairman. In a little over three years, over 3,000 USO clubs opened worldwide. USO programs varied and offered places to relax and socialize. In early 1941, entertainers began performing at Camp Shows at bases throughout the United States. After the United States entry into WWII, the USO expanded their live entertainment to Americans serving overseas. These entertainers endured personal hardships in order to bring their shows to the troops serving overseas. Among those who performed in shows, and made hospital visits were Hollywood stars, June Allyson, Milton Berle and Ann Miller. Bob Hope made his first USO tour in 1942. In the summer of 1944, Bob Hope and his USO troupe visited the southwest Pacific and in August performed in Wakde, in New Guinea. His troupe included stars, Frances Langford, Jerry Colonna, Patsy Thomas and Tony Romano.

By the way, we had Bob Hope's show up here the other day. He had Frances Langford, Jerry Colonna, Patsy Thomas, and Tony Romano with him. They put on a real good show too. They're just the same as they are on the radio, or in the movies. Bob Hope and Jerry Colonna were telling jokes back and forth, and then Jerry also sang a few songs. Frances Langford sang a few songs too, and of course she was real good. Tony Romano sang and played the guitar. I don't know if you've ever heard of Patsy Thomas or not, but boy, was she nice! Bob Hope referred to her as a beautiful hunk of morale, and he wasn't kidding. He said he had her so we could see what we were fighting for. She danced, and then she sang a few lines of his closing song, "Thanks for the Memories." The show lasted for about an hour, and it was real good.

Wakde, New Guinea, **August 27, 1944**

(From the Sven L. Sandstrom collection)
Members of the 342nd Fighter Squadron
taking a rest from working in the hot sun.

Dear "Ginny" -

Hello again, how is every little thing with you these days? I hope you're well. I'm feeling fine and in the best of health. Well I'm answering your letter for July 23rd now. I like this fancy paper that you're using now, with the flower design, or whatever it is, on the upper left hand corner. Some class, I must say. This letter smells pretty nice too. What did you do, put some powder or perfume on it?

Yes, I've heard that Russell is safe, and boy, you don't know how glad I was when I heard that. I really felt "down in the dumps" when I first got his letter back saying that he was missing. He must have had a pretty rough time, and I guess he's had his share. After at least 23 missions that I know of over Europe, being wounded once, then crash landing and being interned, well I guess he's had his share of the war. I guess he'll be all right now though, seeing that he's interned in a neutral country. [8]

I'm glad to hear that Irene[9] made out all right with her baby. I guess she's had a pretty tough time, with losing her husband and everything.

You're not kidding, the war in Europe looks as though it should be over soon. More- so now than when you wrote this letter. Well it can't end too soon to suit me. You asked how the war is progressing over here. Well we're not doing so bad for ourselves. We're getting there slow but sure.

---

[8] My dad's friend, Russell, was interned in Sweden, which was a neutral country during World War II.

[9] Irene was a friend of my mom. She was left widowed with a baby when her husband was killed in the war.

107

We'll be able to do better when the war in Europe is over.

Wakde, New Guinea, September 3, 1944

(From the Sven L. Sandstrom collection)
P-47, "Ginny," Somewhere in New Guinea.

(From the Sven L. Sandstrom collection)
"Babs," the P-47 my dad worked on. Saidor, New Guinea

I'm glad to hear that you liked the pictures that I sent to you, and the one of the plane with your name on it. I'll take good care of "Ginny" for you, but tell your friends that I can't take care of "Babs" for them anymore. That was the plane I worked on, but the pilot has been transferred to another outfit now, and he took the plane with him. I'm working on a different plane now, but the crew-chief hasn't named it yet.

You said you haven't been able to get any film for quite a while now, so you can take some pictures. Well I guess film is pretty scarce now back in the States, because everyone says they have a job trying to get any now-a-days.

Wakde, New Guinea, **August 29, 1944**

(From the Sven L. Sandstrom collection)
Wakde, New Guinea, 1944

So you sent me another box of candy? Well, thank you very much. I hope it gets here in better condition than the last one did. I believe I told you that box was all wet when I got it, and the candy had all melted, so I had to throw it away. When I get this one, I'll let you know how it is. I hope it's alright.

Wakde, New Guinea, September 13, 1944

(From the Sven L. Sandstrom collection)
My dad, (front second from right), singing in a choir in New Guinea.

Did I tell you that I've joined a choir over here? Our Chaplain thought it would be nice to have one, so Kenny and I joined it. It isn't very big as yet, because we just started it a short while ago, but we sound pretty good though.

I don't know if you've heard of these correspondence courses that the government has, but I sent for one of them a couple of days ago. I sent for a course in "Refrigeration." I want to get into "Air Conditioning" as I've told you, but you've got to have a basic knowledge of refrigeration for that, so that's why I sent for that course. I should be getting it in a couple of weeks, so I hope I can learn something from it.

Somewhere in New Guinea, September 21, 1944

(From the Sven L. Sandstrom collection)
Wakde, New Guinea, May 1944

You said you hadn't heard from me for a month. That must have been when I was on my furlough. I didn't do much writing at all then. I guess I only wrote two letters to my mother while I was on furlough. I guess she was worried about me when she didn't hear from me. Well I've been writing to her pretty regularly now, so I guess everything is alright again.

Boy you must have been pretty ambitious to go hiking all weekend. That place that you spoke about must be pretty nice, by the way you describe it. It sounds as though it could be a romantic spot too. Could it? It must be a military secret though, when you only refer to it as a certain spot, on a nice hill. I can't tell very well where the place is by that description.

One day we decided to play some football. Well we played for about an hour straight through and I'm telling you, we were all stiff for about a week after. After that, we decided that this climate over here is too hot to be playing football.

So you felt an earth tremor up there? It's a good thing it wasn't bad so it didn't do any damage. Between floods, hurricanes, and earth tremors, I guess New England has had its share of everything.

Noemfoor Island, September 25, 1944

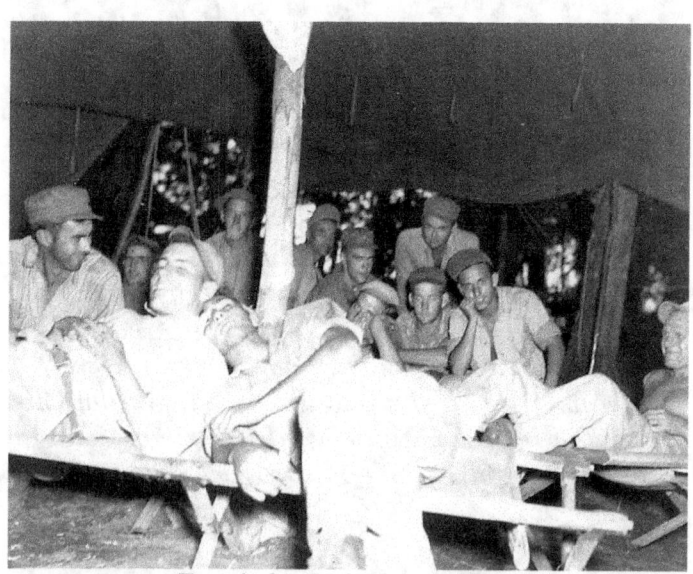

(From the Sven L. Sandstrom collection)
A little down time for some of the men from the 342nd Fighter Squadron.

You asked if I ever got that pin-up of the "Belle Wringer" that you sent. Yes, I received that quite a while ago, and I'm quite sure that I wrote and told you about it. Yes, we have that on one of the planes over here, that's why I took a picture of it. Pretty nice!

Noemfoor Island, September 28, 1944

(From the Sven L. Sandstrom collection)
My dad standing in front of "Belle Wringer."

As a way of expressing individuality and personalizing their machines of war, (in this instance their aircraft), ground crews and pilots would paint words and pictures on the fuselage or nose of the planes. Nose art, which reached its Golden Age during World War II and the war in Korea, was often inspired by wives, girlfriends, and memories of home. Some pilots would name their planes after a loved one at home. Colonel Neel Kearby, Commander of the 348th Fighter Group, named his P-47 *Fiery Ginger* after his wife, Virginia. *Babs*, one the planes my dad was assigned to, was an example of a simple design which displayed only the name. Other aircraft, usually the larger bombers, detailed more elaborate artwork inspired by cartoon characters and pin-ups from magazines and calendars. While nose art was not officially approved or even condoned by the military, regulations were not enforced.

The ground crews logged many hours preparing the planes for each mission. They took pride in the victories won by their pilots. The success of the fighter pilot rested in the faithful and diligent work of the ground crew. They made sure the planes were in proper operational condition and prepared with the armaments necessary to complete the mission. The safe return of the pilot could be attributed not only to his skilled flying, but also to the care with which his aircraft was prepared and maintained. A majority of the artwork adorned by the aircraft was attributed to the talent of the ground crew. In some instances, a squadron was lucky enough to have a talented artist among their crew. Each work of art also depended on available materials.

(From the Sven L. Sandstrom collection)
Col. Neel Kearby's P-47, "Fiery Ginger."

(From the Sven L. Sandstrom collection)

(From the Sven L. Sandstrom collection)

(From the Sven L. Sandstrom collection)

(From the Sven L. Sandstrom collection)

(From the Sven L. Sandstrom collection)
My dad standing in front of a B-24 bomber at Ie Shima

(From the Sven L. Sandstrom collection)
The nose on this B-24 bomber, "Mabel's Labels," displays more detailed artwork.
This picture was taken of my dad while stationed at Ie Shima at the end of the war.

September 2, 1944

20 year old U.S. Naval Aviator and future President George Bush was shot down while on mission to destroy the Japanese radio station on Chi Chi Jima. This island, 600 miles from Japan and 150 miles north of Iwo Jima, was an important military target. The radio station was intercepting U.S. military radio transmissions. Bush's Grumman TBM Avenger was shot down by enemy flak. He was later pulled out of the ocean by a U.S. submarine, while avoiding capture by the Japanese. His crewmen did not survive. A total of 22 American Aviators were shot down of which 8 were taken prisoner. The 8 were later executed and some were cannibalized by high ranking Japanese officers as part of the Bushido warrior indoctrination. This was later ruled as a war crime and those responsible were found guilty and executed by hanging.

I saw a couple of good shows here recently. One was "Two Girls and a Sailor," which was very good, and the other was "What a Woman." That was pretty good too, but not as good as the other one. Have you seen them? I like that new actress, June Allyson, that plays in "Two Girls and a Sailor." She's pretty nice, and I like the way she talks. She has a very pleasing voice, that seems different from the other actresses.

Thanks a lot for the gum that you sent in this letter, it was pretty good. Usually the heat over here spoils gum, unless its wrapped up good, so that you can't chew it, but this was all right.

Noemfoor Island, October 13, 1944

Well here I am again. I'm finally getting around to answering your other letter that I got the other day. I'm sorry I didn't answer it sooner like I said I would, but I've been busy trying to get my first examination finished for my refrigeration course that I'm taking. I just finished it today, so I'm going to send it in now, and then I can get started on my second lesson.

No, I haven't received my election ballot yet, so I don't think I'll bother to vote. I would write for one, but it would be too late by the time I got it anyway. A few of the fellows here have received them, but not too many. So you're going to give me the old one-two if I'm a Roosevelt man, are you? Well I don't think you're big enough for that! You'll have to eat some more "Wheaties" first. As far as politics go though, I won't argue with you on that. There are two things that I don't like to argue about. One is politics, and the other is religion. Boy you're not kidding, I'd like to go down to S.A.C. Park and dance to the good old Swedish songs. I really miss them. You'll probably have to teach me how to do them all over again though, because I haven't done it for so long now. When I was on furlough, I tried dancing a couple of times, but I didn't do so well, so I gave it up as a bad job.

Well "Ginny," this letter should get to you sometime around Nov 6th, maybe a little before, but I want to wish you a very Happy Birthday. I'd like to be there to celebrate it with you, but I guess I won't be. Maybe next year though. I hope so anyway.

Well, I guess I'll close for this time, hoping to hear from you again real soon. Send my best regards to your mother and father.

P.S. Don't forget to vote for Roosevelt now. (or should I say Dewey?)

Noemfoor Island, October 19, 1944

I'm glad to hear that you got a roll of film now, so I'll be waiting to get some more pictures of you. I'll send some more pictures as soon as I get some more film. I've sent home for some, so I hope to get it soon.

I'm glad to hear that you liked the picture I sent home to you. You said it doesn't look as though this climate has gotten me down any. Well, in a way it hasn't, but I don't go for this hot tropical weather all the time. It makes you awfully lazy, and you age faster here than in the States. I guess I can stand it though. I've stood it for seventeen months now, so I guess a little longer won't hurt. After all, you know how tough we Swedes are. (?).

I made up a birthday card for you on a V-Mail form, but I don't know if I can mail it or not. A couple of the fellows were telling me that we're not supposed to draw any pictures or anything on V-Mail to send home. Well I'm going to ask our censor about it anyway, to make sure. If I can't send it, I'll draw it on a separate piece of paper and send it to you anyway, although it may get there a little late.

Noemfoor Island, October 20, 1944

(From the Sven L. Sandstrom collection)

(From the Sven L. Sandstrom collection)

Thanks a lot for the gum you sent in this letter. It tastes pretty good. We've been getting gum here pretty regularly the past few days or so, so you ought to keep this gum for yourself. Now don't think that I don't appreciate it, because I do, but I realize that it's hard to get back in the States too, so you might as well keep what you can get for yourself.

You know, you speak about it starting to get cold back there, whereas over here, we don't even think about that, because it's always hot here, both winter and summer. One thing though, it's going to be nice to get back to those good old New England winters again. I'll probably freeze, but I won't mind that in the least.

Noemfoor Island, November 3, 1944

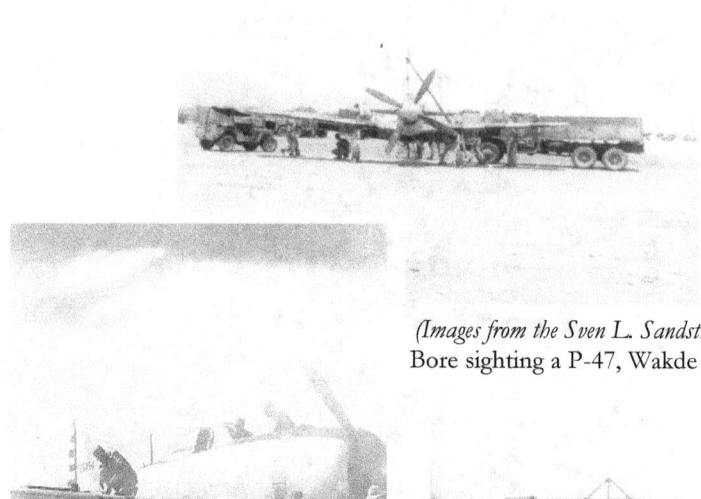

(Images from the Sven L. Sandstrom collection)
Bore sighting a P-47, Wakde Island, 1944.

Caption on back of picture:
Bore sight target on the truck

Bore sighting a fighter plane was one of the most important and painstaking jobs for the armament crew in preparing the plane for combat. The plane was brought out to the firing range where the tail was jacked-up until it was parallel to the ground. The eight .50-Caliber machine guns of the P-47 were mounted parallel to the ground and sighted to a focus point determined by the pilot. The machine guns were usually set to converge at 250 or 360 yards.

The Republic P-47 Thunderbolt (also known as the Jug, short for Juggernaut), was the largest and heaviest single-engine fighter used during World War II. This fighter-bomber, known for its diving speed and firepower, was able to sustain heavy hits from enemy aircraft and still return the pilot to his home base. It was later replaced with the North American P-51 Mustang which had six machine guns mounted on its wings. The 342nd Fighter Squadron began the conversion from the P-47's to the P-51 Mustang aircraft when they arrived in San Marcelino in the Philippines in early 1945.

(From the Sven L. Sandstrom collection)

(From the Sven L. Sandstrom collection)

(From the Sven L. Sandstrom collection)
Noemfoor Island, sometime in the fall of 1944.

(From the Sven L. Sandstrom collection)

> If kisses were like letters, dear,
> I'd send you ten each day,
> To help you fill the empty hours,
> The time when I'm away.
>
> Of course 'it' would be much better,
> If I could have you near,
> Instead I've just a letter,
> I'll send to there from here.
>
> So, each time you receive one,
> please, treat it tenderly.
> Each "billet - doux" I mail you,
> Is a kiss to you from me.

(From the Sven L. Sandstrom collection)
Excerpt from an undated letter
from Somewhere in the Western Pacific.

(From the Sven L. Sandstrom collection)

By early October 1944, U.S. forces began launching air strikes against the Ryukyu Islands, which brought the Allies closer to mainland Japan. In mid October 1944, General Douglas MacArthur returned to the Philippines with his Sixth Army as he had promised when he said, "I shall return," in March 1942 after being ordered by President Roosevelt to leave Corregidor and the Bataan Peninsula. He returned by way of Leyte Island, where the U.S. Navy began waging one of the largest Naval battles in history. The Battle of Leyte Gulf was a decisive U.S. Naval victory, destroying the Japanese Imperial Navy as an effective war machine. It was during this battle that U.S. sailors encountered a new and deadly weapon of the Japanese, the kamikaze attacks. Kamikaze, translated *Divine wind*, were suicide attacks by Japanese military aviators. Using their aircraft as explosive missiles, the kamikaze pilot would deliberately crash into Allied Naval ships resulting in a more death and destruction than conventional attacks. These suicide missions were consistent with samurai life and the Bushido code of loyalty to the Emperor, with death being preferred to defeat. It was considered shameful for the Japanese soldier to surrender or be taken captive, and instead, it was an honor to die for the Emperor. The kamikaze attacks increased through the final stages of the war in the Pacific, reaching their peak in the Battle of Okinawa which began in April 1945.

It was during this time in late 1944 that the 348th Fighter Group was preparing for transfer to their next assignment...

Somewhere in the Philippines.

The Philippines
November 1944 - May 1945

In late November 1944, the 342nd Fighter Squadron transferred to the Philippine Islands. Their first base was in Tacloban, Leyte, and within a short time they were at Tanauan, Leyte.

Dear "Ginny" -

Hello again, and how is the world treating you these days?...We still haven't had any mail in, so I haven't got any of your letters to answer. I hope we get some mail in soon so I'll know what's going on back there, and how everybody is.

I'm sending along a Christmas Card in this letter, and I hope you like it. Our Photo man made up cards like that for the entire Squadron. That's a picture of a New Guinea sunset, and the writing was super-imposed on the picture. (if you know what I mean.) It should say "Philippines" on there instead of "Netherlands East Indies," but they were made up before we moved up here.

Well what's new in Worcester these days, if

anything? Is there anything exciting going on back there, or is it just as dead as ever?

By the way, I see where your favorite (?) candidate was elected President! I bet you were happy to hear that! Well cheer up, maybe next time somebody else will get in, instead of him.

I've been eating some bananas today, the first I've had for quite a while. One of the Filipinos got them for us, and they sure tasted good.

Leyte, Philippines, November 29, 1944

(From the Sven L. Sandstrom collection)

Dear "Ginny" -

Well we finally got some mail in yesterday, and we sure were glad to get it. It's the first we have had now for quite a while. I got two letters from you, and I was sure glad to hear from you again, and that you're all well at home. I'm feeling fine and in the best of health. Well I'm going to answer your letter of October 30th now. Boy, the inside of the envelopes you're using now sure are fancy, with all the pretty flowers and everything.

I got a letter from Gurlie yesterday, and in it was a letter from Russell. I sure was surprised and happy when I got that. He wrote the letter to me, and sent it to her to forward to me. I guess they're treating him pretty good over there, according to his letter, and I'm glad to hear that. I'm going to write him a letter now, and send it to Gurlie so she can forward it to him. He received one of the letters I wrote to him quite a while ago, but they had cut off my return address from the envelope.

Our choir is coming along pretty good. We have about twenty fellows singing in it. We've been practicing some songs for Christmas, for our Christmas Service, for the past few weeks. I guess we'll have a pretty nice Service for Christmas because our Chaplain really puts a lot of work into it. I sent my mother a couple of pictures of the inside of our Chapel, so if you go over to my house and see them, you'll see how nice it is.

Yes, I thought it was a good idea to take up that "Refrigeration" course too, and speaking of that, I got my first examination back from the school yesterday. Believe it or not, I got 100% on it too. I almost fell over when I saw that. I haven't sent in any more lessons yet though, because I've been so busy with moving and everything. I'm going to send one in in a couple of days though. By the way, you'll notice that my address has changed again. It is now A.P.O. 248.

I haven't seen that Abbott and Costello picture that you spoke about, but my mother said she saw it, and thought it was pretty good. Now you say that it isn't any good, so who am I going to believe? If we get it over here, I'll let you know what I think about it. Most of the fellows here would probably like it, because it's a funny picture. We like that type of picture and musical comedies, and things like that, so we can get our minds off of things. One thing we don't like to see over here is war pictures. Of course a few of them are all right, but in most cases, there's too much "flag waving" and stuff to suit me. I'd like to see that picture, "Irish Eyes Are Smiling." I've heard that it's pretty good. We'll probably get it over here sometime, and when we do, I'll be sure to see it. I've heard that song, "Let the Rest of the World Go By," and I like it very much. I think all of them old songs like that are nice.

Leyte, Philippines, December 1, 1944

(From the Sven L. Sandstrom collection)
The Chapel, somewhere in the Philippines

Hello again, and how's the world treating you? I'm feeling fine and in the best of health. Well I guess I'll answer your letter of November 8th now.

I was surprised to hear that the V-Mail card got there on your birthday. I thought it might have been a little bit late in getting to you.

So you were heartbroken because Dewey didn't get in, were you? Well gee, that's tough! Well cheer up. Roosevelt can't win all the time, although I can't see what you have against him. Now I'm not taking any sides for or against any of them, but I'm just interested in your opinions of him. Oh well, who wants to discuss politics anyway? The election is over, and there's nothing we can do to change it.

Well I finally finished up my second examination in my course that I'm taking, so I'm going to send it in tomorrow. My third lesson deals with Elementary Chemistry, so I suppose I'll have quite a job with that, because I never took it up in High School. I guess I'll get it all right though, if I put my mind to it.

Leyte, Philippines, December 5, 1944

Hello again, and how is every little thing with you these days? I hope you're well. I'm feeling fine and in the best of health. I'm sorry I haven't written for the past few days, but we've been pretty busy over here, and I haven't had too much time for writing. We've been putting in twelve and fourteen hours a day at work, so we've been pretty tired at night when we get back to camp, so we usually go right to bed. I started a letter to Russell and Gurlie six days ago, and I just finished it today. I'll write more often from now on though. Not that we're any less busy, but I've got to get caught up on my mail somehow. We haven't had any mail now for a while, so I sure hope we get some soon.

Well I guess I'll answer your letter of November 12th now. First of all, you'll notice that our address has been changed back to A.P.O. 72 again. We haven't moved again or anything, it's just that they changed

December 8, 1944

U.S. Air Force began intensive aerial attacks on the island of Iwo Jima in preparation of U.S. invasion which was scheduled for February 1945.

December 17, 1944

The 509th Composite Group, commanded by Lt. Col. Paul Tibbets was activated. Their assignment was to formulate a strategy for delivering the atomic bomb, which was being development under the Manhattan Project. This group was headquartered on Tinian Island.

February 3, 1945

The battle for Manila in the Philippines began. This battle, which lasted for a month, was the scene of the most violent urban fighting in the Pacific theater, resulting in over 100,000 civilian deaths and total destruction of the city.

it to 248, and then all of a sudden they decided to change it back to 72 again. That's the Army for you. I wish they'd make up their minds.

I don't know what our Group score was the last time I told you, but we've got a few more Jap planes to our credit now. Our Group has 284, and our Squadron is still leading with 126. We've also sunk a few Jap ships, so we're not doing so bad.

You know we're starting on our 20th month overseas today. It doesn't seem so long when I look back on it now, but actually, it has been quite a long time. Like one of the fellows here says, he hopes the next 19 months won't be any less pleasant than the first 19.

You spoke about everything being fine at home, except that Dewey lost the election. Well this same fellow that I just spoke about is a staunch Republican too, and he says that we shouldn't worry, because the Republicans will get in in the next election, and then we can all go home. Well I guess the war can't last forever, and I sure hope it's over soon, so we can all get home again.

I haven't had much time to study the third lesson in my course yet, but I have looked it over and that "Chemistry" sure looks pretty rough. I suppose it won't be so bad though, after I study it enough, and get the general idea of it.

Well, it's getting kind of late, and we have to get up early again in the morning, so I guess I'll close for this time, hoping to hear from you again real soon. Send my best regards to your mother and father.

Leyte, Philippines, December 15, 1944

I just received your letter of November 17th last night, and I was sure glad to hear from you again. We only got a few letters in, and I was lucky to get one from you. It was the only one that I got, and it's the first mail we've had now for quite a while. We should be getting a stack of mail in one of these days, so I hope we get some soon.

You said you hadn't heard from me for over a week. Well I guess that was around the time we were moving, and I wasn't doing any writing. I'm still not writing as much as I should, but I'll get caught up on my mail one of these days, and I'll be able to write more regularly again.

I'm sorry to hear about your brother having ulcers again. I guess it must be pretty awful having them. I hope that diet will cure him again so he'll be all right. I don't imagine that it's much fun living on a special diet all the time. I know it would be kind of hard for me, because I'm a regular "chow-hound." Well I hope your brother gets well again soon.

So you didn't go out with those girls because they were going to a dine and dance joint? Well it's just as well that you didn't go, because that's no place for a girl anyway. It's all right if you're going with a fellow that you know well, but not to go stag.

There's a fellow in the next tent here that's playing his accordion. He's playing a lot of Polkas, and boy, they sure do bring back memories. If I close my eyes, I can just picture myself at the S.A.C. Park or up at the Lodge. By the way, do you go up to the Lodge anymore, or isn't there much sense in going to the meetings now? I remember last year I got a Christmas card from them, and they were telling me about the big party they've got planned for us when we all get home again. I guess that should be a pretty big affair.

Well, we finally passed the three hundred mark in our group now. We now have 304 Jap planes to our credit, and our Squadron is still leading with 139.

Leyte, Philippines, December 21, 1944

Dear "Ginny" -

I just received your letter of Nov. 30th, and I sure was glad to hear from you again. I got your letter of Dec. 14th the other day, and now I get this one of Nov. 30th, so you can see how our mail is coming in. I also got the Christmas card that you sent, and thanks very much for it. It was a real nice card.

I finally received one of my Christmas packages the other day, and it got here in pretty good condition. I hope my others get here just as good. I got some fruit cake, cookies, cheese tid-bits, hard tack, sardines, kippered snacks, and candy. I also got some shaving equipment, tooth paste, and writing paper and envelopes. It was a very nice package.

This noon-time, instead of eating up at the mess hall, the fellows in my tent got together and we made up our own lunch. We had chicken noodle soup, boned chicken, lobster, sardines, kippered snacks, hard tack and bread. We made a pretty good meal out of it, and it sure tasted good. We finished it off with a can of beer, so that made everything complete. A little later on this evening, we're going to make some tea, and have some fruit cake. We have to have our evening snack you know.

(From the Sven L. Sandstrom collection)
Members of the 342nd Fighter Squadron.

We're listening to the radio now and they're playing, of all things, "This is a Lovely Way to Spend an Evening." What a song they pick to play. Oh well, at least it's a nice song anyway. We were listening to Frances Langford singing "Embraceable You" before, and boy, was that nice! She is our female "Swoonatra." She "sends" us the same as Frankie [Frank Sinatra] "sends" the girls. Don't you think she's the appropriate girl singer for that title? At least she fits it better in her class than Frankie does it in his class.

I'm enclosing four pieces of Japanese Invasion money in this letter for you. It's the money that the Japanese used here in the Philippines. One Centavo is worth one-half American cent. At least that's what the Philippine money is based on, so I imagine this is the same.

Leyte, Philippines, January 5, 1945

(From the Sven L. Sandstrom collection)
Japanese Invasion money from the Philippines

Japanese Invasion Money, also known as Southern Development Bank Notes, was issued by the Japanese Military Authority. When the Japanese occupied the Philippines, Burma, Malaya, the Netherlands East Indies, New Guinea, the Solomon and Gilbert Islands, they confiscated all local currency and replaced it with locally printed notes. In January of 1942, when the Japanese captured the Philippines, they used the confiscated hard currency to purchase materials for their war effort. In its place they issued currency in denominations of 1, 5, 10, and 50 centavos, and 1, 5, and 10 pesos. Sometimes referred to as *Mickey Mouse Money*, these notes had no value after the Japanese were defeated. The Japanese were ordered to destroy any bank records and remaining currency before their surrender. Many of the American soldiers collected them as souvenirs, but to this day they have very little value even to stamp and coin collectors.

I got a Valentine's card from my mother the other day, and I sure was surprised when I got that. That was kind of early to be sending them things out. After all, it's almost a month yet, before Valentine's Day. Wait until you see the one I'm going to send to you though. It isn't exactly a Valentine card, but it has the same meaning though. Our photo man was experimenting up in his lab one day, and he made it up and gave it to me. I told him it was just what I wanted, so now I'm going to send it to you for Valentine's Day, and I hope that you'll like it.

We're building an Enlisted Men's Club here now, for the fellows in the Squadron, and it's pretty nice too. There's a stage for the orchestra, a dance floor, and another part where you can write letters, read, play cards, or ping pong. I'm going to try and take some pictures of it when they get it finished, and I'll send them to you, so you can see how nice it is.

I got a Christmas card from Nordic Lodge again this year, and they said they've got $400 saved up toward that "Welcome Home" party they've got planned for us. That must be quite a shin-dig they're going to have. By the way, I asked you last year if you would go to that party with me, and if I remember correctly, you didn't say whether you would or not, so I'm asking again. (on bended knee. Can't you just picture me?!) No kidding though, "Ginny," I would like to have you go with me. Is it a date? (I hope)

I'm enclosing three pictures in this letter for you. One is of me and one of my friends over here, and the other two are just a couple of pictures that are painted on some of the planes here. Don't I look just like a real soldier firing that machine gun? Or do I? The pictures were taken down in New Guinea.

(From the Sven L. Sandstrom collection)
My dad and a friend from his Squadron in New Guinea.

What do you think of the war situation these days? Do you think it will be over soon, so we can all get home again? Boy, it can't end too soon to suit me. We start on our 21st month overseas tomorrow. According to the news, I guess the Yanks are rolling along again over in Europe. I hope they can keep going now until they reach Berlin.

Our boys over here are doing a wonderful job now too, as you can see by the papers. The Navy is really going to town, and they're showing the Nips what they can really do. I only hope and pray that we can keep on doing just as good now, and then we can end this war that much sooner.

Well "Ginny," it's getting along near supper time now, and I've got to get washed and changed before I eat, and then I'm going to church after that, so I guess I'll close for this time.

Leyte, Philippines, January 14, 1945

I'm glad to hear that you're all better now from that cold that you had. Don't forget to take your doctor's advice now, and keep out of any drafts. Look at what happened to me - I got caught in a draft too. (Now don't say what you're thinking. I know that was corny!)

You asked how Christmas was over here in the Philippines. Are you kidding? It wasn't too bad, but then again it wasn't too good either. We spent most of Christmas Eve and Christmas night in the fox-holes, so that didn't help matters any. Oh well, at least it added a little excitement to an otherwise dull evening. (But who likes that kind of excitement though?) We got some of our Christmas packages in yesterday. Kenny got both the one that my folks sent to him, and the one that my brother and his wife sent to him, and I didn't get any at all. How do you like that? Some nerve I must say. It's like I told my mother, I'll probably get my packages in time for next Christmas. I hope I get them soon though, and they'd better get here in good condition too, because I've got some home-made fruit cake, brownies, date squares, and cookies coming from my mother, and I don't want them to get spoiled. After all, I've been sweating them out for quite a while now. I'd also like to get them films that I've got coming, so I can take some more pictures. I guess I'll have to try to borrow a roll from Kenny or somebody, until mine get here.

We got our Enlisted Men's Club completed now, and we had a party in there two nights ago. It sure is a beautiful club, and I wish you could see it. Our photo man took some pictures of it inside, so I'm going to try to get a couple of prints from him as soon as he has a chance to develop them. That probably won't be for a while yet though, but I'll send them as soon as I get them. Well anyway, we had a pretty nice party. There were a few WACs here, and we had a very good orchestra, and then there was a magician too who was pretty good. The fellow who was leading the orchestra used to play at the "Raymore - Playmor" in Boston. You know where that place is don't you? I didn't do any dancing, because I didn't feel like making a fool of myself again on the dance floor like I did when I was down in Australia. I didn't feel much like dancing anyway. A few of the fellows arc up at the club now, dancing with the WACs, but they're dancing to records now. There's one new record that we've got now that is really nice. The name of it is "I'll Walk Alone." They play it quite a lot and I like it very much. I've never paid much attention to the lyrics, but the tune is very pretty. Have you heard it?.

Boy, I agree with you whole heartedly when you say this year will see the end of the war, so we can all get home again. I'm ready to go home any time they want to send me there. I guess I'll have to wait my turn though, the same as the rest of the fellows. Well, we're not doing so bad now over here, so I hope we can keep it up, so we can all get home again soon.

Leyte, Philippines, January 20, 1945

The Women's Army Auxiliary Corps, (WAAC) was created on May 15, 1942, and was given full status as a women's branch of the United States Army in 1943, the Women's Army Corps, (WAC). Modeled after similar British women's units, the Women's Army Auxiliary Corps and Women's Army Corps had about 150,000 women serving during World War II. Up until this time, the only women serving in the military were nurses. Most of the WAC's served stateside, but some were stationed in other places including parts of Europe, North Africa and New Guinea. At first, public opinion was not favorable to having women serve, and in general the men were opposed to women in the military. For some, there was a feeling that women didn't belong in what was generally perceived as a masculine role.

Well I guess I'll answer your letter of Jan. 4th now. You asked if I'm supposed to get a rotation furlough after I've been over here a while. Well that rotation plan states that we are "eligible" for a furlough after we have been overseas for eighteen months, but I guess that's about as far as it goes. We are on our twenty-first month over here now, and there are no signs of any of us going home yet. They'll probably get around to us after a while. It would really be nice to get home again, but I don't know as if I'd like to have to come back overseas again. When I get back home again, I want to stay there, or at least stay in the States anyway, but I guess that remains to be seen. We can just hope and pray that we're all home again soon.

In your last letter, you asked how I spent Christmas Eve, and in this letter you asked how I spent New Year's Eve. Well I told you how I spent Christmas Eve, and New Year's Eve was practically the same. Some fun!!

I was listening to the news on the radio, and they said that the Russians are 170 miles from Berlin now. They advanced over fifty miles in twenty-four hours. They're really going to town over there now again. It was awfully quiet over there for a while, but now that they've started rolling again. I hope they keep it up. After all, the sooner they get the Germans out of the way, the sooner we'll get this war over with too.

Leyte, Philippines, January 22, 1945

(From the Sven L. Sandstrom collection)
My dad in the Philippines, 1945.

We had another party in our club last night, and it turned out pretty good. We had the same orchestra that we had last time. We also had a few more WACs than we had before. You know, they claim that after you've been overseas for as long as we have, in places like New Guinea and the Philippines, that any white girl will look good to us. Well I finally disagree with that statement...I didn't even do any dancing. You probably think I'm crazy for not joining in the dances with the other fellows when I have a chance, but there are plenty of others here that feel the same way as I do. I figure that I've gotten along all right so far over here, that I can wait until I get home again. I don't enjoy dancing anyway, unless I'm with you, Russell and Gurlie and the others at the Swedish dances. Well, we'll get around to that again, when we all get back home.

I'm enclosing that so-called Valentine card that I told you about a short while ago. As I told you, it isn't exactly a Valentine card, but I figure that it's appropriate anyway. I hope you'll like it.

Leyte, Philippines, January 28, 1945

(From the Sven L. Sandstrom collection)

I just received the Valentine card yesterday that you sent to me, and thanks very much for it. It's really a nice card, and I like it very much. That rose on the card sure smells nice. It sort of brings back memories.

I was going to write to you last night, but I just wrote a letter to my folks, and then I went to bed. I was kind of tired, and not much in the mood for writing letters anyway.

One of the fellows here drew my picture two nights

ago, and I sent it home to my folks last night. I don't know if it looks much like me or not, but I think it's a very good drawing anyway. You'll have to go over to my house some day to see it, and let me know what you think of it. This fellow is drawing everybody's picture here in the tent, and he's very good at it too. I hope my picture doesn't get spoiled or anything on the way home.

We're having another party in our club tomorrow night, and I'll write and let you know how it turns out. Maybe I'll try a couple of dances this time, to see how I make out. Well, I'll let you know about it anyway.

Leyte, Philippines, January 31, 1945

Hello again, and how is every little thing with you these days? Good, I hope. I'm feeling fine, but I've got a slight cold.

I'm sorry I haven't written sooner, but as you can see, my address has been changed again. It is now A.P.O. 73. This is quite a place we're at now. In the daytime it's hotter than ---- (well it's hot anyway), and at night it's cold. When we get up in the mornings, it reminds you of a fall morning back home. I guess it must be this changeable weather that gave me this cold. I'm taking medicine and pills for it, so I'll be over it in a couple of days.

Well, I was going to tell you about that party we had in our Enlisted Men's Club. As usual, I didn't do any dancing. On the average, the WACs that we had at that party were a whole lot nicer than those we had the other times. There was one very pretty girl there, and believe it or not, she was a Swede. She comes from Minnesota. I was talking with her for a little while, and boy, what an accent she had.

She sounded as though she just came over from the old country. The orchestra played a polka, but when I got around to finding her again, she was dancing with another fellow, so I was out of luck. All in all, we had a pretty nice party, and we had a good time. It still couldn't compare to the dances we used to go to back home though. I'll enjoy myself when we get back to them again.

Somewhere in the Philippines, February 8, 1945

I just received your letter of Jan. 14, and I sure was glad to hear from you again.

You spoke about that being one of those stormy days, that I perhaps have almost forgotten about. Well, I suppose it would feel kind of strange to me to see some snow again, because it's been almost two years now since I've seen any. I'd like to be there and roll around in some of them snow drifts, just to see how it feels. I'd probably freeze though after being so used to this warm weather for so long now. I'd still enjoy it very much though. I wouldn't let a little thing like that bother me, if I could be there again.

Boy, you're not kidding, we get pretty tired after a twelve or fourteen hour day on the "line." We don't usually work that long now though. We put in about nine or ten hours a day now. Last night though, we didn't get back from work until a quarter of nine, and I sure was tired when we got back here to the tent again, because we were really busy all day long, loading bombs and guns, after they got through bombing and strafing. When I came back to the tent here, I went down and took a shower, changed cloths, read my mail, and then went to bed.

February 6, 1945

Over 500 Allied POW's were released when U.S. Rangers raided a POW camp in the Philippines.

February 19, 1945

U.S. Marines began the invasion of Iwo Jima. The capturing of this island along with its three airfields was important as part of the strategic attacks against mainland Japan. Halfway between the Marianas and Japan, Iwo Jima would provide an emergency landing site for damaged B-29's returning to the Marianas from bombing missions over Japan. Iwo Jima also provided a base for short-range fighter escorts. The Marines quickly captured Mount Suribachi, but it would be a month of intense fighting before they would capture the island.

I was surprised to hear that Barbro has signed up with the Navy. I suppose she's going to go in as a nurse isn't she? I hope she makes out all right in it.

Somewhere in the Philippines, February 18, 1945

So you wish that they could add on a couple of more hours every day, do you? Well I don't know as if I'm inclined to agree with you on that or not. I believe that days are long enough as it is now. In fact, sometimes they seem to be too long to suit me. The only time they're not long enough is on my day off. I plan to get caught up on my writing and study my lessons, and stuff like that, and I don't seem to get any of it done.

You asked if I got any more Christmas boxes. Yes, I finally got some. I received one from Tangrings, one from my aunt and uncle, and then I got one from my mother and father the other night. That makes four that I've received so far now, and I've got about ten more on the way, that I know of. I'll probably get them in time for next Christmas. I received those five rolls of film from my folks, that I told you about, so now I'll be able to take some pictures and send to you. I should have some for you in a couple of days or so, and I hope they come out good.

I can just imagine how surprised that girl was when her brother came home from the Marshall Islands. I know just how he must have felt too, to get home again after two years. That's sure going to be a happy day when I pull into Worcester again. I don't know when it will be, but I hope it's soon. Will you come dashing out of your office in a split-second too, to meet me?

I'm enclosing a couple of pictures for you in this letter. They are the pictures of the Enlisted Men's Club that I told you about. I told you it was a beautiful place, and now you can see that I wasn't kidding. One picture is of the bar, and the other is of the dance floor and band stand. All of the pictures on the walls were painted by the same fellow that drew my picture that I sent home to my folks.

The pictures behind the band stand are the New York skyline, the Squadron insignia and the Golden Gate bridge. The picture behind the bar is our old Group Commander's ship, "Fiery Ginger." You've probably heard of him. His name was Col. Neel Kearby, and he had twenty-one Jap ships to his credit when he went down. If you'll look close in the picture, you can see the twenty-one Jap flags painted along the side of the cock-pit, just like he had on his own plane. The bombs hanging down from the ceiling had lights in them, so it gave an indirect lighting effect. (Ultra modern, you know!) Well, I hope you like the pictures.

Somewhere in the Philippines, February 22, 1945

(From the Sven L. Sandstrom collection)
Enlisted Men's Club in the Philippines.
Picture of Col. Kearby's P-47, "Fiery Ginger."

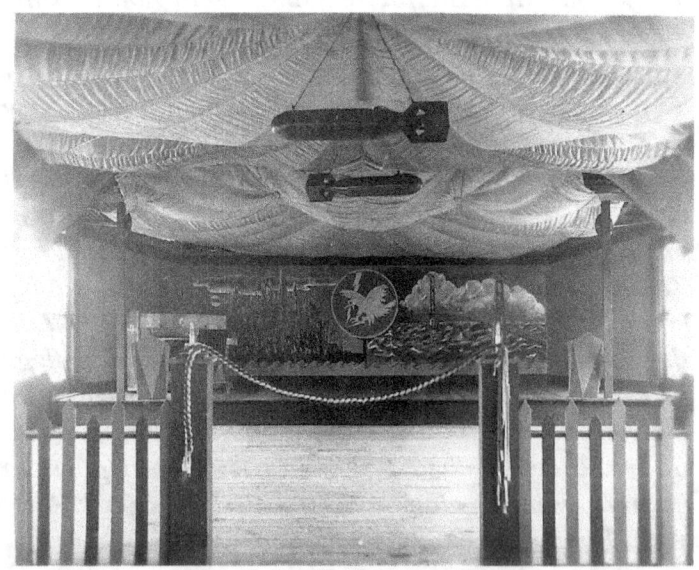

(From the Sven L. Sandstrom collection)
Picture of Enlisted Men's Club
showing the dance floor and band stand.

You're not kidding, the war is moving right along now, and I hope and pray that we can keep it up now. What did you think of the news of all them Navy planes that have been bombing Tokyo? I sure was surprised when I heard that on the radio. I never thought that our Navy would get in that close to Japan without getting into a fight, but that's all that much better that they can. Boy, I sure hope that we can get this war over soon now, so that we can all get home again. Well, I guess we'll make out all right. No, I did not see any of those American prisoners that were released from the Jap prison camps. I can just imagine how happy they must have been when that happened. I imagine they will have a lot they could tell about, but usually them fellows don't like to talk about it. It was the same in the last war too. The fellows that saw action didn't like to talk about it, whereas those that didn't see any action, talked as though they had won the war themselves. Well anyway, I believe them American prisoners deserve a good long rest now, after what they've been through.

Somewhere in the Philippines, February 25, 1945

I heard about that snow storm that you had back there. I don't know if I told you or not, but my mother sent me a whole page out of the "Gazette," showing different views of the city after the storm. That snow was really piled up in places too. My mother was saying that the drifts were as high as she is tall, in our driveway. I thought that winter that I spent at Bedford was bad, but I guess this one was worse, according to what everyone says.

I'm glad that your cousin, Bob was able to get home, and I can just imagine how glad you all were to see him again. I bet he must have felt pretty good too, to get home again. I can assure you it's going to be a wonderful feeling for me to get home and see you and my folks again. I've often thought about how I'd feel, and what I'd say, and everything, but I guess that's pretty hard to tell. Well, I hope the day is soon when I can be back home again.

I'm certainly glad to hear that you'll go to that "Welcome Home" dance with me up to Nordic Lodge. I guess it will be, like you say, a super-duper affair from the way they explained it to me. You said you hadn't heard anything about it before. Don't you go to the meetings anymore? I can't say as I blame you any for not going, because I don't suppose there's much doing up there now. I guess I'll have to write them a letter one of these days, because I haven't written to them for quite a while now. Well don't forget that's a date now, and I also hope to have many more besides that one.

Somewhere in the Philippines, March 5, 1945

Dear "Ginny" -

I'm awfully sorry that I haven't written for the past few days, but I got a couple of days off and I went to Manila , so I haven't done any writing.

No doubt you've read about how Manila was destroyed, in the papers back home. Well we read about it too in our news sheets, and we also heard about it on the radio, but you can't even begin to imagine how much damage was done unless you can see it for yourself. Boy, I thought the damage we had back home after the hurricane was bad, but that doesn't even come close to comparing with this. I took a few pictures while I was down there, and if they come out good, I'll send them to you, and then you'll be able to see a little bit of what it looks like. One of the rolls that I used didn't roll up right on the spool in the camera, and when I opened the camera to put in a new roll, I think I got some light on it, so I don't know if it's going to come out or not. I'm having our photo man develop it anyway, because probably the first few pictures will be all right. I hope so anyway.

I'm going to try to go there again someday, and then I'll take some more pictures too. I'll also get something to send to you....We went in to one store to buy some kind of an embroidered table cloth, or something, but she wanted too much for it. We tried to get her to lower the price, but we weren't getting very far, so we gave it up as a bad job. I guess we must have talked with her for about an hour and a half. She was the first Filipino that I've met that used our so called slang expressions. Usually they speak more or less a refined English, pronouncing every syllable and word very plain, whereas this girl talked just the same as you or I, or anyone else back home, using different expressions and phrases, etc. that are common among Americans. I don't know if that's very clear or not, but you probably know what I mean.

Well anyway, she told us a joke. It's very corny, but never-the-less it's pretty good. - A woman went into a butcher shop, and asked for a yard of pork. Now she wanted to know if we knew what she meant when she said that. Well we racked our brains for a while, but we couldn't figure it out, so we asked her what it was. So then she told us that a yard of pork is three pig's feet. (Pretty corny, huh?)

There's quite a lot that I could tell you about that place, but that would take an awful lot of writing. I'll be able to tell you about it better anyway, when I get home again.

I'm enclosing a picture for you in this letter, that our photo man took of me the other day. As you can see, I'm very hard at work on my new plane. By "new plane" I mean we have P-51's now, instead of the P-47's. Personally I like the '47's better, but this is really a very good ship too. Well I hope you like the picture.

Somewhere in the Philippines, March 13, 1945

(From the Sven L. Sandstrom collection)
Caption on back of picture:
This is yours truly, hard at work on my airplane. Don't I look it?
- Philippines, March 1945 -

I received your letter of Feb. 22nd and I sure was glad to hear from you again. You said that you were feeling pretty good for an old lady. Gee whiz, what makes you feel so old all of a sudden? Don't tell me that you're working so hard these days that it's getting you down? You'd better take it easy and relax for a while. You'll have to feel like a "spring chicken" when I get home again, because I'll be wanting to take you out most every night, and you'll

(From the Sven L. Sandstrom collection)
Caption on back of picture:
Me and Ed Holmes

(From the Sven L. Sandstrom collection)
Caption on back of picture:
This is my airplane that I work on. P-51 Mustang

have to be able to stand the late hours. (I'm wondering if I'll be able to stand it.) I'm used to going to bed fairly early every night now, but I wouldn't mind staying up late every night just to be with you, and my folks again. Well, I guess we'll make out all right.

Boy, here it is March 22nd already. I started this letter on the 18th and this is as far as I've gotten. I didn't have time to finish it the night that I started it, and on the next night I sat down to write and for the life of me, I just couldn't think of anything to write about. The next night we had a physical exam and a Squadron meeting after that, so when we got through with them, it was too late to do any writing. Last night I sat down to write, and I was in the mood to write a lot of letters. I just about got started going good, when my Flight Chief came in and told me that we had to go down to the "line" and work on some airplanes. Well, we got back here at a quarter to twelve, so I just washed up and went to bed. Now tonight we were required to go over to the movie area and listen to a talk by one of our group officers, and now we just came back a few minutes ago, so now I hope I can finish this letter without being disturbed anymore.

My mother sent me some pictures that she took around my yard after that big snow storm that you had back there. Boy, there sure was a lot of snow around there. There was one picture of my old Plymouth standing in the yard, and the snow was right up to the roof on one side of it. That poor old car isn't getting any care at all now. I doubt very much if it will ever run again, so I guess I'll have to bring it up to Linder's Junk Yard when I get home again. He'll probably give me around ten dollars for it anyway.

I'm enclosing pictures for you that I took when I was in Manila. They're not very clear, but at least you can get a faint idea of some of the damage that was done.

Somewhere in the Philippines, March 18, 1945

The following pictures were taken in Manila and are part of the collection of pictures my dad sent home to my mom in March 1945. These pictures show some of the destruction following the month-long battle of Manila which began on February 3, 1945.

(From the Sven L. Sandstrom collection)

(From the Sven L. Sandstrom collection)
One of the docks in Manila Bay, 1945

(From the Sven L. Sandstrom collection)

(From the Sven L. Sandstrom collection)

(From the Sven L. Sandstrom collection)

I'm finally getting around to answering one of your letters that I got the other day. I'm sorry I haven't written sooner, but I've been pretty busy the last couple of days. I made up an Easter card on a V-Mail form and sent it to you, so I hope you get it all right. I don't know if they photograph V-Mails with pictures on them anymore or not, so I colored the picture in case they didn't photograph it. Well, you can let me know if it gets there. Last night I went to church to celebrate Holy Communion. I was going to go tonight too, for the "Good Friday" service, but we had a Squadron meeting and church was all over when we got through with that. We've got a Sunrise Service on Sunday morning, and then our regular service on Sunday night. Our Chaplain sure had a lot of work to do this week to prepare all of them services.

A couple of the fellows in my tent here just came back from Manila, and of all things, they brought back a "Monopoly" game with them. Remember when that game used to be so popular a few years ago? I guess we'll have to play that one of these nights, to pass the time. We used to play it quite often at home, and I think it's a lot of fun.

I haven't seen that picture, "So Proudly We Hail," that you spoke about and I don't know as if I'd really care to. Of course, it's probably a good picture, and all that, but I don't enjoy these war pictures very much. I like to go to a show to forget about the war, and get my mind off things. All the fellows feel the same way too, so that's why we'd rather see good musical comedies, and pictures of that nature. They ought to send more of them over here, and never mind the others, but I guess we have to take what they give us, and be satisfied.

That must have been quite a broadcast that you heard from Iwo Jima. I remember when we were still in New Guinea, right after the Philippine Invasion, we were getting broadcasts of that same type from Leyte. It does make you feel as though you're right there, but, you can't imagine what it's really like, unless you go through it yourself. I've never been through anything that rough, but I've been through plenty of bombing raids, and that's plenty rough enough for me. I really sweat them out every time. Oh well, one of these days we'll all be back home again, and we can get back to normal. (Oh Happy Day!).

Yes I heard that Paul Holst is missing in action, and I sure hope that he's all right. At least there's hope for him when he's listed as missing, because he might be a prisoner of war, and the prisoners over in Germany are treated fairly decent anyway.

I got a letter from my mother today, and she said she was over to the store and she saw Mr. Tangring when she was there. She asked him how Gussie was, and he said that he just called up to say good-bye because he was going across. I don't know where he was stationed, so it's hard to tell whether he's coming over this way or if he's going to Germany. It would be nice if he could get stationed over here, somewhere near me, but I guess that remains to be seen. Well, where ever he goes, I hope he makes out all right.

So, you're having your house painted now, are you? I bet it will look nice when it's all finished. I guess your father must have had quite a job trying to find a painter these days.

Somewhere in the Philippines, March 30, 1945

(From the Sven L. Sandstrom collection)

I went to the show again last night and saw "Girl Rush," with Frances Langford. I didn't care for it at all, so I walked out on it.

Well I came back from the show, and three of us here in my tent decided to play some "Monopoly" to have something to do. The game only lasted about two and a half hours, and believe it or not, I ended up with all the property on the board, plus a couple thousand dollars in cash besides that (big business!) It was a lot of fun, but now the fellows are out to get my neck the next time we play. We'll probably play again tonight when we get back from church, but I'm not sure yet. Well I guess I'll answer your letter of March 8th now.

I'm glad to hear that you got that Valentine that I sent to you and that you liked it. No, I didn't make it up myself. One of the fellows in the photo lab made it up, and when he got it finished he showed it to me. I liked it very much, so I asked him to make me one, because I wanted to send it to you. He made that the same time he was making up the Christmas cards, so I saved it for Valentine's Day, because I thought it was very appropriate for then. Of course, you understand what it says on the card is true at all times, but I just waited for Valentine's Day so that I would have something to send to you.

Somewhere in the Philippines, April 1, 1945

Hello again, how is everything with you these days? Good, I hope. I'm feeling fine and in the best of health. I received your letter of March 13th, and I sure was glad to hear from you again.

I was going to write to you last night, but I didn't even get a chance to get started, when the fellows decided to play Monopoly. Well, there was so much noise that I couldn't even concentrate so I decided that I might as well join in the game too. I was the second one to go broke, and then it was so late that I just went to bed.

We went to the show again last night too, and then I was going to write as soon as we got back here to the tent. Well tonight there are only two of us here, and it's nice and quiet, so we're both trying to get caught up on some of our mail. I've got so much mail to answer though, that it's going to take me quite a while to get around to them all. I try to write to you and my folks first, and then write to the others, when I have any spare time. I'm getting them all answered slowly but surely though.

161

March 9-10, 1945

Over 300 B-29's left the Marianas; destination Tokyo. The B-29's carried out low-altitude bombing raids, dropping incendiaries over Tokyo, destroying approximately 16 square miles of the capital and killing an estimated 100,000 civilians in what would become the single deadliest bombing mission in the war in the Pacific.

April 1 -June 21, 1945

The Battle of Okinawa, codenamed Operation Iceberg, was an 82 day-long battle characterized by fierce fighting and increased intensity of kamikaze attacks. This fighting resulted in the largest numbers of causalities in any battle in the Pacific theater. Capturing this island gave the Allies airfields only 350 miles from mainland Japan. Okinawa would be the staging point for the planned invasion of mainland Japan scheduled for November 1, 1945.

What do you think about the war news these days? Pretty good, eh? I'm sweating out that war in Europe now, and it shouldn't last too much longer, the way our boys are really going to town over there. Who knows, maybe it will be all over by the time you receive this letter. That sure would be nice. After that's over, then we can concentrate everything over here, and get this war over with in a hurry too. It can't be too soon to suit me. Well, I guess I'll get around to answering your letter now.

You know, this letter of yours sure smells nice. It looks as though you put some perfume or something on the corner of it. Did you?

You said that you were listening to some of the pre-war records up at Barbro's house. Well I agree with you, you can't beat them songs, because they're really nice. We have a radio program over here that's on every evening, and they play a lot of them old songs, and some semi-classical songs *too. It's nice to listen to them songs while writing letters. I know that your favorite orchestra is Glenn Miller, and he's my favorite too, although Sammy Kaye runs a pretty close second. I used to enjoy his "Sunday Serenade" program that he used to have. I don't know if he still has it now or not, but he had a real nice program though. You've probably heard it at some time or another.*

Boy, Arthur Stenstrom sure was lucky to get home on furlough. He came over here quite a while after I did, but of course he's in the Navy, and I don't know how they work out their furlough. Well, I guess some fellows have it, and some don't. I'll probably get around to having a furlough one of these years too. It can't be too soon to suit me.

You asked if I could tell you exactly where I am. Well, I'm sorry. I'd like to tell you, but the censorship regulations state that we can only say, "Somewhere in the Philippines." I don't know why, but I guess they must have their reasons. We can't even tell any of the places where we were in New Guinea either, and that's all past history by now. Well, I'll tell you all about it when I get home again, as to where I've been, and what I've seen, etc.

You're not kidding about Iwo Jima. I guess it must be pretty rough on the fellows up there. I don't know as if I'd like to be stationed there. The only place I'd like to be stationed at now, is back in good old Worcester, - on Greenwood St. Well, I hope it won't be long before I'm back there again.

Somewhere in the Philippines, April 3, 1945

I finally received the Christmas package that you sent (at long last), and thanks very much for it. It was really swell. Everything came in good condition, except the candy and cigarettes. The cigarettes were stale, and the candy was all melted together, but the rest of it was in very good condition. Kenny said to thank you very much for what you sent to him too. He appreciated it very much. He's been having some trouble with his stomach lately, so he's in the hospital now, getting a physical check-up. I guess he'll be all right in a few days.

Well, I went to see that picture that I told you about, "Here Come the Waves." I thought it was a fairly good picture. At least it was entertaining anyway. It was supposed to be a "dig" at Frank Sinatra, more or less. Bing played the part of a nationally famous "swoon king," and whenever he sang, he had all of the girls swooning and fainting, like they do when "Frankie-Boy" sings. Betty Hutton played a dual role. She was supposed to be twin sisters. In one part she was a sweet, demure young lady, and in the other part, she was one of these girls that faints all the time when Bing sings. It wasn't too bad a picture, although they over did it in some parts.

I received a little package from Norton's today. They sent me one of their sharpening stones, and I sure was surprised to get it. I guess I'll have to write and thank them for it. I haven't written to them for quite a while now, so I guess I'll have to get on the ball.

I also received another package from my mother. She sent a big fruit cake, and the surprising part of it was that it came in perfect condition. It had about three separate cardboard boxes and wrapping paper on it, so that's why it didn't get spoiled. It really tasted good too.

Remember in my last letter I told you that we were not allowed to say exactly where we are, or where we've been? Well they just came out with a new censorship regulation, and now we can tell where we've been, but we still can't give our exact present location. It seems funny that they should come out with that, right after I get through telling you that we couldn't write about it. I guess they're getting a little more lenient in their censorship rules now. We can't tell you when we were at the different places, or the order in which we were there, but you don't want to mind that. I can tell you all about that when I get home again.

Well anyway, here's a list of the places we've been, and you can figure out for yourself approximately when we were there. As for New Guinea and the Netherlands East Indies, we were at Port Moresby, Wakde Island, Saidor, Hollandia, Finschhafen, Dobodura, and Noemfoor Island. Up here in the Philippines, we have been at Tanauan, Tacloban and San Pablo on Leyte, and as I've told you before, I've been to Manila. Where we are now is a "military secret," but I'll be able to tell you that later on sometime. That will give you a brief idea as to where I've been, but of course there's a story that goes with each place, and I can't tell you about that right now. I'll be able to tell you all about it someday, and also about my trip "across" and everything.

Somewhere in the Philippines, April 6, 1945

In February 1945, the Big Three leaders, President Roosevelt, British Prime Minister Winston Churchill, and Soviet Premier Joseph Stalin met at the Yalta Conference in the Crimea. The purpose of the conference was to discuss policies and plans for the final stages of the war, including the occupation of Germany and re-establishment of war-torn European nations. This was the second of three major conferences during World War II that were attended by the top leaders of the Big Three Allied nations, (the first was the Tehran Conference of 1943 and the third was the Conference at Potsdam in July 1945).

At the time of the Yalta Conference, the Allies were on the verge of victory in Europe. The Germans were retreating to Berlin, where the Soviets were advancing towards what would become the final major offensive of the war in Europe. The U.S. and Great Britain saw a protracted fight in Japan and looked to the Soviet leader to enter the war in the Pacific. The Soviet Union agreed to enter the war with Japan three months after the war in Europe ended. Stalin's conditions were recognition of Mongolian independence from Nationalist China, and Soviet influence in Manchuria including their railways and the strategic seaport, Port Arthur. Roosevelt agreed with the hopes that the United Nations [10] would deal with this issue.

Upon his return to the States, Roosevelt's failing health was quite apparent. Since the beginning of his unprecedented fourth term as president, the longest running presidency in history, the years of his struggle with polio and stress from the job had taken a terrible toll on his health. He retreated to his vacation home on top of Pine Mountain in Warm Springs, Georgia where he would rest before he was to appear at the United Nations Conference on International Organization in San Francisco. On April 12, 1945, at the age of 63 years, President Roosevelt died suddenly and unexpectedly of a massive cerebral hemorrhage.

In his four terms as president, Roosevelt lead the United States through the dark days of the Great Depression and now was just a few months from leading the nation towards victory in World War II. Within a few hours of his death, Vice President Harry S. Truman was sworn into office as the 33rd president of the United States.

---

[10] The United Nations was established in 1945, replacing the League of Nations which was seen as ineffective since the end of the first world war. On April 25, 1945, the UN Conference on International Organization met to begin drafting the United Nations Charter. President Roosevelt, who coined the name, was scheduled to attend this conference.

I received your letter of March 23rd, and I was sure glad to hear from you again.

Last night we saw "Bring on the Girls," with Veronica Lake, Eddie Bracken, Sonny Tufts, and Marjorie Reynolds. That was a real good picture too. They had Spike Jones in the picture too, and his band played, "Chloe." Boy, did we laugh at that. He has a swell arrangement of that song. You might say that it's silly, but he specializes in that type of music, and he puts it over good. At least it's something different for a change anyway.

We heard of the President's death over the news, and that sure came as a surprise to us. It sure is tough to lose him. It's too bad that he couldn't have lived a little while longer, so that he could have seen the end of the war anyway, but I guess it was his time to go, and there's nothing that anybody can do about it. Well, I hope that President Truman does a good job now.

Somewhere in the Philippines, April 15, 1945

(From the Sven L. Sandstrom collection)
American Red Cross Club in Manila

Well here I am, way behind in my letter writing again, as usual. I'm sorry I haven't written for the past few days, but I had a pass to go to Manila, and I just got back from there. I didn't do any writing at all while I was there, because there wasn't any place for me to mail my letters anyway, so I hope you'll forgive me. Thank you, dear, I knew you would!

I bought you a couple of more souvenirs while I was there. It isn't much, but at least it's something anyway. I got you four fancy colored handkerchiefs, and also a handbag. I believe the handbag is made out of pineapple or something. They dry out the strands of the fruit some-how or other, and then they weave it together. It doesn't look too bad, but you can judge that for yourself when you get it. I'm going to send it in a couple of days or so, as soon as I can get them wrapped up and censored. I hope they get there all right, and that you'll like them.

I didn't buy too many souvenirs when I was there because most of their prices are too high. I guess it's the same in all foreign countries though. They think that all Americans are millionaires, and so they raise their prices when they see us coming. And of course, being the "suckers" that we are, we pay them and let it go at that.

I guess I did more walking while I was there than I've done since I got overseas. We walked all over the city, looking at all the different sights, and also looking for souvenirs at the same time. We were out morning, noon, and night, just walking around. (My poor feet!) It was worth it though, to see all of the places that had been ruined, and also the places that weren't touched at all. We got around to see more of the city this time, than I saw the first time I was there.

We were talking with an American who has lived in the Philippines for the past twenty-eight years. He was a prisoner of the Japs for quite a while, and he told us some of the things that they did. Some of the things they did weren't too bad, but then too, some of the things weren't too good either. I guess it must have been pretty rough.

Somewhere in the Philippines, April 25, 1945

I just got back from the show a little while ago. The picture was so bad that I had to walk out on it. The name of it was "Tahiti Nights," with Jinx Falkenburg. They must think that we're a bunch of morons or something according to some of the pictures they send over here to show us. Once in a while they have some good shows, but most of them are real "stinkers." And that isn't only my opinion either. Practically all of the fellows think the same thing. They'll probably get around to showing us some good pictures one of these days. Well, I guess I'll answer your letter of April 3rd now.

So you finally went over to my house and saw the pencil sketch of myself that I sent home? I see that you agree with me, that it doesn't look too much like me. It does have a faint resemblance in some places but that's about all. I don't know how soon it will be before I send home the colored sketch. You see, the fellow that's going to draw it is in the hospital now, and I don't know how soon he'll be back again. He was having some trouble with his stomach, so they sent him to the hospital to get it fixed up. I'll get him on the ball as soon as he gets back again, and have him draw my picture.

By the way, as you can see, my address is now A.P.O. 74. We are still in the Philippines though, and I guess we'll be here for a while. At least I hope so anyway, because it gets pretty tiresome moving around all the time. There is one move I won't mind making though, and that is the move back to Greenwood St. again. I sure hope that it's soon.

Somewhere in the Philippines, April 26, 1945

Hello again, and how is every little thing with you these days? Good, I hope. I'm still alive and kicking. We've been quite busy here lately, so I'm slightly worn out. Our pilots are bombing and strafing every day, so that keeps us hopping all the time. It gets pretty tiresome, but I guess that's to be expected. Today is my day off, so I can rest up a little bit, but I've got so many letters to answer, that I guess I'll be busy writing all day.

By the way, have you been to any dances lately? I suppose S.A.C. Park will be opening up for the summer pretty soon now. I'd like to be there to go to some of those Swedish dances with you. Maybe I will be. Who knows? It's possible, but I don't know how probable. Well no matter when I get back, it's still going to be nice just to see you again, and I'm not kidding. Well I hope that it's soon too. Well I guess I'll answer your letter of April 6th now.

First of all, thanks a lot for the picture that you sent in this letter. It's really swell, and you look wonderful. I'm glad to hear that you got another roll of film so that you can take some more pictures too. I enjoy getting them. I haven't finished my roll of film yet, but I'll get around to it one of these days.

How are you coming along on your scrapbook that you're making of all the pictures I've sent to you? You said that you've got quite a collection already.

(From the Sven L. Sandstrom collection)
Preparing to load a bomb on a P-47.
These bombs, which weighed about 1,000 pounds each, would
require a team of about 5-6 men to load them onto the aircraft.

(From the Sven L. Sandstrom collection)
P-47 taxiing out to run-way to take off.
These two pictures, both taken in New Guinea,
were enclosed in the letter dated April 29, 1945.

Well I haven't got any more pictures of myself right now to send to you, but I've got some others that I can send to you to add to your collection. They're probably not very interesting pictures, but I'll be able to tell you all about them when I see you again. I'm enclosing a couple for you in this letter, that were taken down in New Guinea when we had the P-47's. One picture shows a bunch of the fellows getting ready to load bombs, and the other shows one of our planes taxiing out to the run-way to take off. You'll notice that there is a bomb hanging from the belly of the plane. I'll send you some more pictures in my letters until I run out of them. Well "Ginny," I guess I'll close for this time, hoping to hear from you again real soon. Send my best regards to your mother and father.

I'll be seeing you.
Love,
Lou

Somewhere in the Philippines, April 29, 1945

Dear "Ginny" -

Hello again, how is everything with you these days? Good, I hope. I'm still kicking around as usual.

Remember that picture "National Velvet" that you told me about in one of your letters? Well believe it or not they're showing that picture here tomorrow night. I almost fell over when I saw that listed. I'll write and let you know what I think about it when I see it. They've also got another picture coming this week that I want to see. The name of it is "Music For Millions," with Margaret O'Brien and June Allyson. The main reason I want to see it is because June Allyson is in it, and she's my favorite actress now. The first time I ever saw her was when we saw "Two Girls and a Sailor," down in New Guinea, and I took a liking to her right away. I believe all of the fellows here like her a whole lot better than Gloria DeHaven, who played in the same picture. It might have been just that part that she played in the picture, but she caught everyone's fancy over here. Cute kid!

I received your letter of April 15th and I sure was glad to hear from you again. Thanks very much for the picture that you sent in your letter. That's really a wonderful picture of you, Bobby, and your folks. You all look real good. Bobby sure has grown up a lot, hasn't he? Boy, the way these kids are growing up back there, I won't even know them when I get back again.

One of the fellows in the tent here just decided to have some pop-corn, so he got out a can of it that he had received from home, and we popped some. That's the first time we've had any of that for a long time now, and it sure tasted good. We'll probably brew up a little cocoa later on, and have some sardine sandwiches or something, and some fruit cake. We usually have something to eat every night in the tent here before going to bed. We're just a bunch of chow-hounds, I guess.

Somewhere in the Philippines, *May 2, 1945*

Remember that picture, "Music for Millions" that I told you about? Well I don't know as if they're going to have that show here or not. It was listed on our movie schedule at the beginning of the week, but I haven't seen it listed at all since then. You see, we have a little news sheet, "The Bomb Daily," that we get every day and they list all the movies in that,

(From the Sven L. Sandstrom collection)

and where they're playing. I haven't got any of them right now, but I'll get one for you and send it in my next letter so you can see what it looks like. Well anyway, I hope they get that picture, because I'd like to see it.

You said you saw some newsreels of Manila. Well that gives you a faint idea of what it's like. It looks worse when you actually see it though, than it does in pictures. Do you remember what parts of the city they showed? It must have been around the business district, the "Walled City," and the bay, because they were damaged the most. It's a shame they had to destroy it, because it looks as though it must have been a beautiful city before the war. I guess it will take them quite a few years to get it cleaned out and built up again. A fellow could come over here after the war and make a good living in all the industries and everything that they have to build up again. There'll be an awful lot of opportunities for the right men, but that's not for me though. I want to settle down in the good old U.S.A. again, and stay there. I've had enough of these foreign countries to last me for a while.

I'm enclosing two more pictures for you in this letter. They were both taken when we first came to the Philippines. You can see some of the mud that we had to go through. Some fun!

Somewhere in the Philippines, May, 4, 1945

(From the Sven L. Sandstrom collection)
Pictures enclosed in letter dated May 4, 1945. Taken somewhere in the Philippines, these pictures show the flooding and mud the soldiers encountered.

Those engaged in the battle of the Pacific from the middle of 1944 and into the spring of 1945, saw some of the most fierce fighting in the war. Capturing the Marianas and Iwo Jima came at a heavy price in terms of Allied casualties. This brought the Allies within striking distance of mainland Japan, where bombing missions were planned using the highly sophisticated Boeing B-29 Superfortress. There was a major shift in the tactical bombing from high altitude precision bombing to low altitude incendiary bombing. Taking off from major airfields in the Marianas, the B-29's carried out their missions, dropping incendiaries on major cities in Japan, including Tokyo. The bombing of Tokyo on March 9-10, 1945, codenamed Operation Meetinghouse, resulted in a firestorm leaving an estimated 100,000 civilians dead and approximately 16 square miles of the city burned to the ground. The fire bombing raids continued through July and by the end of the campaign, most of the major cities of Japan had been destroyed with millions of civilians left homeless.

In the spring of 1945, the Battle of Okinawa was underway. Capturing Okinawa would be of strategic importance as the staging point of the planned full-scale invasion of mainland Japan later that year. The Battle of Okinawa, the largest of the Ryukyu Islands, was the scene of the most deadly fighting in the Pacific. After 82 days of brutal fighting, under terrible conditions, more than 12,000 U.S. soldiers and Navy personnel were dead or missing in action, with another 36,000 wounded.

While stationed in the Philippines in early 1945, the armament crews of the 348th Fighter Group were logging many long hours preparing the P-51 Mustangs with bombs and ammunition. The Mustang pilots were flying as many as 200 sorties a day, breaking records, including dropping a greater tonnage of bombs in a single month than any single heavy bomb group. In close support of the infantry, the 348th pilots hit many types of targets including caves, entrenchments, barges, and factories. They earned the reputation of a "go down and blast 'em" scourge of the Japanese. [11]

---

[11] From the Fifth Air Force Press release, early June 1945. See page 184.

Victory in Europe,
As the Pacific War Continues
May 1945

In Europe, Hitler's Third Reich was rapidly falling apart in the early months of 1945. Hitler had retreated to his Führerbunker in Berlin in January, and the leaders braced for what would be the final confrontation with the Allies, the Battle for Berlin. On April 29, 1945, Hitler learned of the execution of Italian Dictator Benito Mussolini and his mistress Clara Petacci by Italian partisans. After the execution, the corpses of Mussolini, Petacci, and twelve other executed Fascist leaders were hung up by the heels where they would be reviled, stoned, shot at, and spat upon in an act of revenge, and warning to any other Fascists who might continue to fight. On April 30th, Adolph Hitler commit suicide in his Führerbunker in Berlin. He shot himself in the head while his wife, Eva Braun (whom he married the previous day), commit suicide by ingesting cyanide.

On May 7, 1945, the Allies formally accepted the unconditional surrender of the armed forces of Nazi Germany and Adolph Hitler's Third Reich. This brought an end to the war in Europe. May 8th became a day of celebration known as Victory in Europe Day or V-E Day.

Well how did you like the news of Germany finally surrendering? We had been expecting it for quite a while, so it wasn't a surprise, but it was still great news. I only hope and pray now that we can finish up this war over here in a hurry, so we can all get back home and back to normal again. I don't believe it will take too long, once we get all of our forces over here. We'll be able to go to work on Japan in earnest then. I'd hate to be in their shoes.

I suppose Russell will be coming home on furlough now pretty soon. I hope so anyway, because he really deserves one, after what he's been through. I guess most of the fellows in Europe will come over to this theater via the States, so they can have a furlough first. That's no more than right though, because they've been through quite a lot over there, and they've done a wonderful job. Maybe when we get some of them men over here, they'll give us a break, and send us home. I hope so anyway, because after all, two years away from home is an awful long time. Well I guess we'll have to wait and see.

Remember quite a while ago I wrote and told you that our squadron broke the world's record in the number of enemy planes shot down? Well last month we broke another world's record. Our group dropped a greater tonnage of bombs in one month than any other outfit has done. That is, for a fighter outfit, of course. I don't know if we're allowed to say how much we dropped, but I'm going to find out, and if we can, I'll let you know in one of my next letters. If we can't, then I'll be able to tell you all about it when I see you again.

Luzon, Philippine Islands, May 11, 1945

Well, I suppose you're beginning to think that I've forgotten all about you by this time, aren't you? Well I haven't. I'm sorry I haven't written for so long, but we've been pretty busy, and then I went to Manila for three days besides that.

In the first place, we just got through moving, and it took us a few days to get set up and organized. We didn't have any lights set up so we weren't able to do any writing at night. We had to work all day, and by the time we got through washing up and eating, it was too dark to do any writing. I just came back from Manila yesterday. I was on a three day pass. I was going to write to you last night, but they had a movie by the War Dept. that we were all required to see so now I'm finally getting around to writing to you tonight. I hope you'll forgive me for the delay. Thank you dear, I knew you would.

Today was the first time we had any mail for quite a while, and I didn't get any letters from you. I haven't heard from you for quite a while now. I hope you're not sick or anything, and that everything is alright. I hope I hear from you soon.

I suppose you've heard about the "point system" they're going to use to discharge soldiers now, haven't you? Well that isn't going to affect me in any way, because I've only got 79 points, and you're supposed to have at least 85. We have four battle stars now, and there's a chance that we might get either one or two more, but we're not sure yet. If we do get them I'll have either 84 or 89 points, but I'm not worrying about that any.

We just learned now, that fellows in the Air Corps have to have at least thirty months overseas before we're even eligible for rotation or furlough back to the States. I've got twenty-four months to my credit now, so I've got at least six more months to "sweat it out." Oh well, I'll be home again one of these years.

Luzon, Philippine Islands, May 24, 1945

I just received your letter of May 16th and I sure was glad to hear from you again. It's the first letter that I've had from you in quite a while, so I'd been wondering if anything was the matter. I'm glad to hear that you're well, and that everything is all right. I'm still alive and kicking, and working just as hard as ever.

Joe E. Brown was here Sunday night with his show, but I didn't go and see it. I was going to go to church instead, but I missed that too. We didn't get back from the "line" until it was quite late, and by the time I had washed up and eaten, it was too late to do anything, so I just wrote a letter instead. I broke a record yesterday by answering three letters. That's the first time I've written that many for I don't know how long. I'm getting so I can only write one or two letters at the most every day. I guess my mind is going blank on me, because I just can't seem to think of anything to say. (And no remarks, either!) Of course there's a lot that I could write to you about, but I'll have to tell it to you personally, when I see you again. I don't think it would make very interesting writing. You see, it primarily concerns my post-war plans, etc., if you know what I mean. Do you think you'll be interested to hear about it when I get home again? I hope so.

You asked what I thought about the war in Germany being over. Well it sure was great news and I was glad to hear it, but we didn't do any celebrating. I guess there wasn't too much celebrating anywhere, as far as that goes. We still have them d--- Japs to contend with and after we've licked them, then I'll be happy. I guess they'll get their bellies full as soon as we get all of our forces over here, and start pounding them in earnest. According to the news, the B-29's are doing a pretty good job on them now. I'm glad I'm not in their shoes. I'm just sweating out when they start them thousand plane raids over Japan night and day, and then we'll see how they like that. You'd think they could read the handwriting on the wall by now, but I guess you can't expect much from a bunch of fanatics like them.

Luzon, Philippine Islands, May 28, 1945

(From the Sven L. Sandstrom collection)
My dad in front of the 342nd Fighter Squadron sign. Each Japanese flag represents a Japanese plane shot down by the pilots of the squadron. San Marcelino, Luzon, Philippine Islands, 1945

We have a speaker set up in our tent now, that's hooked up to the squadron radio, so we listen to that while we're writing letters. There's one song in particular that they seem to be playing quite a lot lately. The name of it is "Don't Fence Me In." It's really a nice song and I like it.

I was just listening to the news, and they just said that the B-29's have destroyed fifty-one square miles of Tokyo. Boy, oh boy, that sure is a lot of damage to do to one city. They claim that it is no longer an important military target. Them B-29's have certainly done a wonderful job. Just wait until they can have thousand plane raids day and night over Japan, then just think all the damage they'll do! I hope them Japs soon realize what they're in for, and they give up. That will make me very happy.

I'm enclosing a bracelet for you, in this letter, so I hope it gets there all right. It's made out of some shells that we got when we were down in Wakde Island. The catch or snap, or whatever you want to call it that I've got on there isn't very good, so what you should do is bring it to a jeweler or something, and have them put a good one on there. I hope you'll like it.

Luzon, Philippine Islands, May 30, 1945

Hello again, and how is every little thing with you these days? Good, I hope. I'm still alive and kicking, and working just as hard as ever. Well yesterday we started to drive on the right hand side of the road for the first time in two years. We've been driving on the left hand side of the road all through New Guinea and the Philippines up to now. It seemed kind of strange to get back to the right way of driving again, but still it felt pretty good too.

I went to the show tonight and saw "Meet Me in St. Louis," with Judy Garland and Margaret O'Brien. I suppose you saw that picture when it was in Worcester didn't you? It wasn't too bad a picture, but it wasn't all that it was cracked up to be. We got rained out near the end of the picture, so I didn't see the whole show. Our sound system wasn't working too well tonight, so that might have been one of the reasons I didn't enjoy the picture too much. There was an awful lot of noise and everything, and you couldn't even recognize Judy's voice when she was singing, so that spoiled it. Oh well, all in all, it wasn't too bad, I suppose.

Remember that song "One Meatball" that you told me about in one of your letters a while back? Well I heard it for the first time last night. It sure is a silly song. I heard Bing Crosby singing it. He also sang another song that I think is very nice. The name of it was "I'm Making Believe." It's songs like that that I like to hear, and that goes for most of the other fellows too. We're just a bunch of sentimentalists, I guess. (or something.)

I'm enclosing a press release for you in this letter, that was distributed to the squadron today. They sent this story to all the newspaper syndicates in the States, so you'll probably be reading it in the Telegram or Gazette.

That little squadron insignia on the bottom of the page is an "extra added attraction" that I put on there for you. What do you think of the 348th now? Pretty good, eh? Now you can see what I mean when I told you that we've been pretty busy lately. That makes a lot of work for the armorers, and I'm not kidding. Well at least I did some good anyway, so that's some compensation.

Luzon, Philippine Islands, June 2, 1945

1. THE FOLLOWING IS A PRESS RELEASE ISSUED BY FIFTH AIR FORCE
   TO ALL CORRESPONDENTS:

   "FIFTH AIR FORCE, PHILIPPINES--- FOR THE FIRST TIME IN
   THIS WAR A FIGHTER GROUP HAS DROPPED A GREATER TONNAGE
   OF BOMBS DURING A SINGLE MONTH THAN ANY SINGLE HEAVY
   BOMB GROUP.

   THE RECORD SHATTERING OUTFIT IS THE FIFTH AIR
   FORCE FIGHTER COMMAND'S 348TH FIGHTER GROUP. DURING
   THE PAST MONTH, P-51 MUSTANGS OF THIS JAP BLASTING
   FIGHTER GROUP DROPPED 2091 TONS OF BOMBS, OF WHICH
   2068 TONS WERE CHECKED OFF AS DIRECT HITS ON PIN-POINT
   TARGETS.

   THE 348TH, WHICH DURING ONE PERIOD SHOT DOWN
   231 JAP AIRCRAFT FOR A COMBAT LOSS OF ONE PILOT, HAS
   BEEN CREDITED BY GROUND FORCES INTELLIGENCE WITH THE
   DESTRUCTION OF 10,000 JAPANESE BY BOMBING AND STRAFING
   DURING THE PAST MONTH.

   DOING THEIR BOMBING "ON THE DECK" IN CLOSE
   SUPPORT OF INFANTRY DIGGING THE JAPS OUT OF LUZON, THE
   348TH'S PILOTS DID SUCH OUTSTANDING WORK, OFTEN AS
   CLOSE AS 50 YARDS IN FRONT OF AMERICAN LINES, THAT THE
   GROUP HAS BEEN OFFICIALLY COMMENDED BY THE COMMANDING
   GENERALS OF THE 38TH INFANTRY DIVISION AND 112TH CAVALRY.

   FLYING AS MANY AS 200 SORTIES A DAY, THE
   MUSTANG PILOTS FIRED NEARLY 2,000,000 ROUNDS OF .50
   CALIBER AMMUNITION DURING THE PAST MONTH. THEY STRUCK
   EVERY CONCEIVABLE TYPE OF TARGET — CAVES, ENTRENCHMENTS,
   GUN EMPLACEMENTS, TROOPS, VEHICLES, FACTORIES, WARE-
   HOUSES, BARGES, SHIPPING, AND ANYTHING ELSE THAT WAS
   JAP. THEY DID THE JOB WITH THE LOSS OF A SINGLE PLANE,
   AND THE PILOT OF THAT ONE WAS RESCUED.

   THE 348TH FIRST ESTABLISHED ITS REPUTATION AS
   A "GO DOWN AND BLAST'EM" SCOURGE OF JAP SHIPPING. IT
   RAN UP A RECORD TOTAL DURING THE LEYTE CAMPAIGN AND
   DURING ONE THREE WEEK PERIOD THIS YEAR ITS PILOTS SANK
   ONE TENTH OF THE JAP SHIPPING CREDITED TO THE ENTIRE
   FIFTH AIR FORCE."

(From the Sven L. Sandstrom collection)
Press release issued in early June 1945, by the Fifth Air Force
regarding the success of the 348th Fighter Group.

I got a letter from my mother, and she said that Russell is on his way home. I sure was glad when I heard that. She also said that Harry is on his way home on furlough again too, because he had just come out of the hospital. Maybe they'll both be able to see each other. That would really be nice. I'd like to be there too, but I guess I'll have to wait until after the war is over, and we're all home for good. That's going to be a happy day, and I'm not kidding. I hope that day isn't too far away. The boys in the tent here are making some tea now, so we're going to have some tea and fruit cake before going to bed. We usually have some little snack like that every night before we go to bed. (It makes us sleep better!)

Luzon, Philippine Islands, June 14, 1945

On February 26, 1942, by Executive Order 9075, the Presidential Unit Citation, (originally known as the Distinguished Unit Citation) was established. It was awarded to a unit that "displayed gallantry, determination and *esprit de corps* in accomplishing its mission under extremely difficult and hazardous conditions so as to set it apart from and above other units participating in the same campaign." The PUC was worn on the right side of the uniform before all other unit citations. Additional PUC awards were denoted by oak leaf clusters.

Our group has been awarded the Presidential Unit Citation for the work that we did in New Guinea. I believe we'll get an Oak Leaf Cluster for it too, for the work we did up here, but that hasn't come through yet. That doesn't give us any more points towards discharge, but at least it's a ribbon to show for the work we did. We wear that ribbon on our right breast instead of the left, so you can always tell a soldier that has earned that citation.

I don't know if I told you before or not, but I got a letter from my mother, and she said that Russell's folks got a cable-gram saying that he was on his way home. I sure was glad when I heard that, and I bet his folks and Gurlie are all excited about it. Harry is coming home too, on a rest leave, so I hope they can both be there at the same time. That would be nice if they could see each other. I'd like to be there to see them too, but I guess I'll have to wait until the war is over for that. I understand that Gussie is down in New Guinea now, so maybe he'll be coming up this way soon. I hope so anyway, because I sure would like to see him again. He's probably at some replacement camp now, waiting to be assigned to some group. I guess I'll just have to sweat it out though, and see where he gets stationed. I hope its somewhere near me. My mother sent me a clipping out of the paper, and it had my picture there and it told all about me being in the Philippines. I almost fell over when I opened the letter and saw that. I don't know why she had that put in the paper, but I guess it's all right.

(this letter was closed with...PS. I may not be able to write for a couple of weeks or so, so if you don't hear from me, you'll know why. Love Lou.)

Luzon, Philippine Islands, June 21, 1945

Well here I am, finally getting around to writing to you again. I'm sorry I haven't written any lately, but I told you in my last letter that I wasn't going to be able to. I guess I'll be writing regularly from now on though.

I got a letter from my mother and she said that Gussie is down in New Guinea now. I sure was surprised to hear that. I hope he gets sent up around here someplace now, so that we can see each other. I don't know exactly where he is down there, because I haven't got his address as of yet. It probably wouldn't do any good to know where he is anyway, because I couldn't get way down there to see him. We'll just have to wait and see if he gets stationed up here. I just got a letter back today that I had sent to my brother, Al, last April. He was in California at the time, so I guess he must be overseas by now, or at least on his way over here anyway. On the envelope it said that he had left there and didn't leave any forwarding address. Well I hope he gets sent over around here someplace so that I can see him. It's been over two and a half years now since we last saw each other, so that would be quite a reunion. The best reunion of all though is going to be when we all get together again for good, and I hope that day isn't too far away. They could send me home right now if they wanted to, and I wouldn't mind it one bit.

Luzon, Philippine Islands, July 8, 1945

This was the last letter sent from the Philippines. The 348th Fighter Group moved and began operations on Ie Shima, an island next to Okinawa in the Ryukyu Islands on July 12, 1945. Censorship regulations became more strict. The letters my dad sent in July were undated and headed with "Somewhere in the Western Pacific."

Dear "Ginny," -

I'm sorry I haven't written for the past few days, but as you can see, my address has changed again. It is now A.P.O. 245. We're not allowed to say where we are, and we can't even put any dates on our letters, but they'll probably let up on the censorship rules pretty soon.

I received a letter from my mother one day, and Russell had written a few lines to me while he was still in Sweden. He had to send that letter through

Gurlie, so that's why it took it so long to get here. Well anyway, it was really swell hearing from him again, and I sure was glad to hear that he finally got home. I guess he just missed seeing Harry by about a week or so. You should get a chance to see him anyway, because he'll be home for two months. They say that he looks real good. I believe my father got a film, so he's going to take some pictures of him and Russell to send to me. I hope he sends them soon because I'm anxious to see how they both look.

So your sister finally had her baby? Well I'm glad to hear that they're both doing well. My sister, Virginia and my sister-in-law are both expecting the stork to visit them too, but I don't know when. I think my sister expects hers around the latter part of Sept., but I don't know when Helen is expecting hers. I hope one of them gets a girl. After all, I've got a couple of nephews now, and I'd like to have a niece. I suppose that remains to be seen.

Somewhere in the Western Pacific, Sometime in July

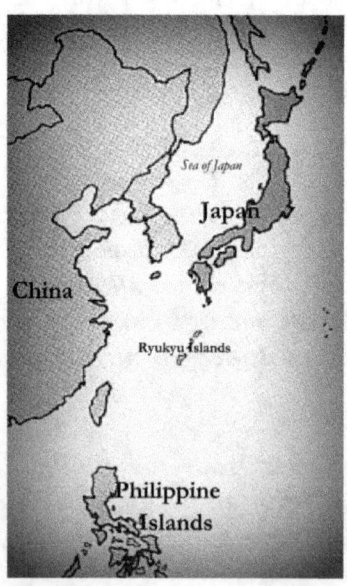

(From the Sven L. Sandstrom collection)
"Million Dollar Hill," Ie Shima, 1945

(From the Sven L. Sandstrom collection)
Ie Shima, 1945

I got a letter from Nancy Tangring and she sent me Gussie's address. I sure was glad to get it, because now I'll be able to write to him. It's been a long time now since we last wrote to each other, so it will be nice to hear from him again. He's down in New Guinea, as you probably already know. I know exactly where he is by the A.P.O. number. I don't suppose I could mention it in my letter though, because the censor would probably cut it out anyway, so we'll let it go at that. I'm going to write to him in a day or two now, and see how he is.

Boy, I probably won't even recognize Greenwood Park when I see it again, by the way you describe it. They've sure made an awful lot of changes up there. I believe they took the band stand down before I left there, or at least they were starting to tear it down anyway, because the hurricane ruined it. I wonder if they'll ever build another one up there. I believe they should, because it used to be nice to go up there in the evenings and listen to the concert.

Somewhere in the Western Pacific, Sometime in July

Hello again, how is every little thing with you these days?.

We finally got some mail in today, but not very much. I only received one letter, but it was equal to a dozen letters, because it was the one that all of you wrote in when you had that party over at my house. I sure was surprised to get that letter. Boy, I sure wish that I could have been there too, but we'll have our good times when we all get together again. I'm glad to hear that you had a good time over there. It's pretty hard to explain exactly how I felt when I was reading that letter, but there was a slight touch of home-sickness involved in it. That may sound silly or something, but as I said, it's pretty hard to explain it. You probably know what I mean though. I could just picture the bunch of you over there, and then I got to wondering how nice it's going to be when we all get back there again. I get into them moods every once in a while, and then start thinking about home, but I suppose that's only natural.

We've started to send fellows home on the point system, and also some on T.D. (Temporary Duty). This T.D. is nothing but a forty-five day furlough at home, and then they send you back overseas to your outfit again. As far as the point system goes, I don't imagine I have much of a chance on that, because you have to have at least 85 points to be eligible for that, and I've only got 79. They said they're going to lower the score in a couple of days or so, but I doubt if they'll lower it too much. If they lower it to 79 or less, I suppose I might as well wait until they get down to me, then go home for discharge. Otherwise, if they offer me a chance on T.D. I think I'll take it. I'd hate like heck to have to come back over here again after I ever get back to the States, but at least I'd have a chance to be home for a few days anyway, and there's nothing I would enjoy more than that. I don't know if I explained that very clear or not, but what's your opinion? I wrote and asked my mother and father about it, and I'd like to know what you think about it too. It might be a couple of months or so yet, before they get around to asking me if I want to accept it or not, but when and if they do, I'll let you know about it.

I had quite a dream the night before last. I dreamed that I was home and that I was over to your house, visiting you. Harry Steemson was there with me, although I don't know how he happened to be there. Well we were talking for a while, and then you asked me why I never told you that I loved you. I made some kind of excuse that I thought was understood. Then, of all things, you asked me to marry you. I don't know what made me dream like that, because I didn't have anything like that on my mind before going to bed. It was a nice dream though.

Somewhere in the Western Pacific, Sometime in July

(From the Sven L. Sandstrom collection)
"Our planes wrecked by a Jap bomb one night." Ie Shima, 1945

(From the Sven L. Sandstrom collection)
"Hauling away our wrecked planes." Ie Shima, 1945

On July 16, 1945, the world's first atomic bomb detonation, the Trinity test, took place in Alamogordo, New Mexico, after U.S. scientists worked on its development in the top secret *Manhattan Project*. A few days later, President Truman approved the order to use the atomic bomb in the war. In mid July, the Big Three Leaders, Truman, Churchill and Stalin, met at the Potsdam Conference where a declaration was issued, calling for the complete and unconditional surrender of the Japanese government. The Japanese rejected the declaration on July 28th.

Towards the end of July the censorship regulations changed again:

I just received your letter of July 6th and I sure was glad to hear from you again. We just got some more mail in, and I received ten letters, so that boosted my morale a few points.

As you can see, I've got the date on this letter. We haven't been allowed to put it on our letters before this, but don't ask me why, because I don't know. It's just that the base censor wouldn't allow it, and we have to abide by their regulations. Some of their rules and regulations sound awfully silly to us at times, but I suppose they know what they're doing and who am I to question them.

I received some pictures from my mother that were taken down at my brother-in-law's farm. My mother, father and brother have a vegetable garden down there, so they sent me some pictures of that. It showed them working in the garden too, so I told them they all look like a bunch of farmers now.

Ie Shima, July 25, 1945

Well, I've got a surprise for you, if you want to call it that. Remember I wrote and told all about the point system and T.D. and I asked your opinion about it? Well yesterday I made up my mind as to what I want to do. I don't know what you're going to think about it, but I think that you'll probably agree with me in my decision. I've thought it all over carefully, weighing both sides of the question, and I've decided to take T.D. if they will let me have it. I went up to see the Adjutant yesterday and asked him to put my name on the list. That doesn't mean that I'll get it though, just because I applied for it. It is now up to the discretion of our Commanding

Officer as to whether he wants to give it to me or not. We could ask for any month that we wanted, so I asked for next month (August). That doesn't mean that I'll get it either. They may wait until Sept. or even Oct. before they'll let me go. There are about five or six of us that have asked for it for August, so I think there's a fairly good chance that we'll get it. Don't go getting your hopes up or anything, because as I said, it's up to our C.O. to decide if he wants to send us home or not.

Both the point system and T.D. have their advantages and disadvantages, so as far as I can see, it's only a matter of your own personal opinion, as to what you think you'd rather have. One of the other fellows here that's applying for it too, has the right idea I think. He says that we've got the opportunity of going home for forty-five days, and we'd be crazy not to take it, considering that we've been overseas for over two years now and we haven't got enough points for discharge. There's no doubt that it would be nice to get discharged, but when I came into the Army, I was told that I'd be in for the duration plus six months, so I can't see where I'm losing anything. In fact I've got everything to gain by being able to go home for a month and a half.

I don't know how soon it will be before we know anything definite about it. It may take a couple of weeks, maybe more, or maybe less. You see, if our C.O. approves it, the papers have to go to Group Headquarters, then to Fifth Air Force Headquarters. Then they go back to Group again, and finally back to our squadron. Sometimes they can send the papers through in a matter of days, and sometimes it takes a couple of weeks. I'll just have to sweat it out now and see what's what.

Ie Shima, July 29, 1945

Victory in Japan
August 1945

Early in 1945, plans were underway for making what would have been the largest amphibious invasion in the history of warfare. Operation Downfall was the codename for the planned, full-scale invasion on mainland Japan. Downfall, which consisted of two phases, was scheduled for later that year. Phase one, Operation Olympic, would be the assault on the southern island of Kyushu, and was scheduled for November 1, 1945. It would have involved all available Allied forces already in the Pacific. Okinawa would be used as the staging point. The second phase, Coronet was scheduled for March 1, 1946, using Kyushu and Okinawa as the staging area for the invasion of the Tokyo plain, Honshu. Troops used for Coronet would have come from reserve and redeployed troops from the European war.

By the summer of 1945, with a stronghold on Iwo Jima, the Marianas and the Ryukyu Islands, as well as redeployed troops from the war in Europe, the Allies were poised to begin phase one of this massive invasion on mainland Japan. It was expected that Operation Downfall would be met with great opposition, not only by all available organized military in the Japanese Empire, but also by the fanatic and extremely hostile civilians. Some estimated that the Allied casualties would mount to anywhere from 500,000 to over a million.

In July of 1945, as the 348th began operations from Ie Shima, in the Ryukyu Islands, preparations for the invasion were being made. My dad and his squadron were only a short distance from mainland Japan, on a small island next to Okinawa. Meanwhile, preparations were being made for a different mission on another island; Tinian Island, in the Marianas, approximately 1,500 miles south of Japan.

On August 5, 1945, the first operational atomic bomb, codenamed Little Boy, was loaded onto a B-29, Enola Gay, on Tinian Island. Sometime around mid-night on August 6th, a pre-flight briefing was held and at 2:45 A.M. the Enola Gay, took off with its 12 man crew, piloted by Col. Paul Tibbets. Little Boy was armed while in flight, and shortly after 9:00 A.M., the bomb was released from Enola Gay. Little Boy exploded as planned almost 2,000 feet above its target, Hiroshima, and yielded more power than 20,000 tons of T.N.T.

In a White House Press release, dated August 6, 1945, President Truman announced the dropping of this first atomic bomb on Hiroshima, while appealing to the Japanese Empire to surrender: "It was to spare the Japanese people from utter destruction that the ultimatum of July 26 was issued at Potsdam. Their leaders promptly rejected that ultimatum. If they do not now accept our terms they may expect a rain of ruin from the air, the like of which has never been seen on this earth. Behind this air attack will follow sea and land forces in such number and power as they have not yet seen and with the fighting skill of which they are already well aware."

Three days later, in the early morning hours of August 9, 1945, a second B-29, Bockscar, left Tinian Island loaded with a plutonium-type atomic bomb, codenamed, Fat Man. The primary target, Kokura, was under a cloud cover making it difficult for the bombardier to view the aiming point. The decision was made to divert to the secondary target, Nagasaki, and at around 11:00 A.M., Fat Man was dropped. This second atomic bomb yielded similar results as the earlier Little Boy on Hiroshima. On the previous day, the Soviet Union declared war on Japan, effective on the 9th. Soviet and Japanese hostilities resumed with the invasion of Manchuria.

I was going to write to you last night, but the news came over the radio that Japan was willing to accept our surrender terms, and I just got so that I couldn't do any writing or anything else.

I'm telling you, I was so happy and excited, that I couldn't sit or stand still. We kept moving back and forth to the radio, listening for any new developments. Of course, we've got to wait and see now what our military leaders are going to say about it, and whether they're going to accept it or not. I'm just hoping and praying for the best now.

I had just started a letter to my mother last night when the news came over. I didn't feel like writing after that though, so I let it go until tonight, and I just finished the letter now.

I don't suppose there's much sense in talking about the news, because by the time you get this letter, it will be old stuff anyway. Maybe I'll be home for Christmas this year after all. Who knows? That sure would be nice, and I'm keeping my fingers crossed.

Ie Shima, August 11 , 1945

August 15, 1945, (August 14 in the United States), six days after the bomb was dropped on Nagasaki, Emperor Hirohito announced in a radio address that his people should accept the surrender. He blamed their defeat on the use of a "a new and most cruel bomb" which was unleashed on Hiroshima and Nagasaki. On that day, President Truman announced in a White House press conference that the Japanese had surrendered; "This is the day we have been waiting for since Pearl Harbor. This is the day when Fascism finally dies, as we always knew it would." Americans declared August 14th V-J Day or Victory in Japan Day.

Dear "Ginny" -

Hello again, how is every little thing with you these days? Good, I'm glad to hear it. I'm feeling pretty good myself, especially now that Japan has finally accepted our surrender terms. That sure made me a happy boy, and I'm not kidding.

There wasn't too much noise when the news came over the radio. Of course we were all mighty happy about it, but that's about all. There was more cheering going on the first night the news came over the radio that the Japs were willing to accept our terms, but even that didn't last too long. I expected to hear a lot of shouting and hollering, but I see I was mistaken. Well, I'm just waiting now to see how long it will take them to send us home. I haven't the slightest idea as to how long it will take, but it can't be too soon to suit me. As soon as I hear anything about it, I'll let you know. I doubt if it will be for a while yet, but of course that's something that you can't tell about the Army. They're worse than women when it comes to changing their minds.

Ie Shima, August 17, 1945

On August 19, 1945, a delegation from Tokyo was sent to meet with General Douglas MacArthur in Manila to work out the details of the Allied occupation of Japan as well as the terms of surrender. Two B-25's of the 345th Bombardment Group and several American P-38's escorted two Japanese Mitsubishi G4M-1 Betty bombers, carrying the Japanese envoy. The two Betty bombers, named Bataan 1 and Bataan 2, were painted white with green crosses on the wings, fuselage and vertical tail surfaces, as a sign that they were carrying the delegation and were on a peace mission. The members of the delegation arrived at the airstrip on Ie Shima, transferred to a USAAF C-54 transport, and were flown to Manila where they met with

General MacArthur. There were still some hard-line Japanese military leaders who did not support the surrender. Consequently, the Betty bombers were under heavy guard both in the air and on the ground out of fear that some Japanese military might attempt to stop or shoot down the planes and prevent the surrender.

We had a Thanksgiving Service in church this morning for the Victory over Japan, and then we had Holy Communion after that. We had a very nice service. Our Chaplain was back with us again, after having been in the hospital for two weeks. It was nice having him back with us again.

Well, they've relaxed on the censorship a little bit now, so we can tell you exactly where we are. I am not in Okinawa as you thought I was, but I'm right next door to it, on Ie Shima Island.

We had an important event take place on this little island today, as you no doubt read about in the papers or heard on the radio. The Japanese envoy from Tokyo stopped at this island on the way to Manila to confer with Gen. Douglas MacArthur. They came here in a couple of Jap planes, then transferred to one of our transports to take them the rest of the way to Manila. They broadcast the whole thing on the radio, and they took newsreel pictures of it too. They broadcast it around 12:30 P.M. noon today here, so it was heard in the States last night (August 18th) around 11:30 P.M. We saw the planes flying over here. It sure was a wonderful sight.

I bet that girl in your office was pretty surprised when she found out that her father had been working on the Atomic Bomb. They sure kept that a secret from everybody. I'm certainly thankful that it was our country that discovered that, and not the Japs. That would have been a real calamity.

I hear they have a new bathing suit back in the States now that the girls wear. They call it a "MacArthur Suit," because it's guaranteed to land any man on the beach. (corny, isn't it?)

Ie Shima, August 19, 1945

(From the Sven L. Sandstrom collection)
Two Japanese "Betty" bombers carrying the Japanese envoy to Ie Shima.
Picture is taken from one of the two B-25 escorts. (August 19, 1945)

(From the Sven L. Sandstrom collection)
One of the "Betty" bombers landing on the airstrip at Ie Shima

(From the Sven L. Sandstrom collection)
Japanese "Betty" bomber landing on Ie Shima

(From the Sven L. Sandstrom collection)
Japanese "Betty" bomber carrying the envoy, with two Japanese pilots.

On September 2, 1945, the Japanese Empire formally surrendered aboard the U.S.S. Missouri, anchored in Tokyo Bay. General Douglas MacArthur, Supreme Commander for the Allied Powers, gave the introductory statement, "We are gathered here, representatives of the major warring powers, to conclude a solemn agreement whereby peace may be restored. The issues, involving divergent ideals and ideologies, have been determined on the battlefields of the world and hence are not for our discussion or debate... The terms and conditions upon which the surrender of the Japanese Imperial Forces is here to be given and accepted are contained in the Instrument of Surrender now before you."

The Instrument of Surrender was prepared by the War Department and approved by President Truman. The second of eight paragraphs from the document stated: "We hereby proclaim the unconditional surrender to the Allied Powers of the Japanese Imperial General Headquarters and of all Japanese armed forces and all armed forces under Japanese control wherever situated."

Once the signing was complete, General MacArthur concluded, "Let us pray that peace be now restored to the world and that God will preserve it always. These proceedings are closed!"

Although some mark this date in history as the end of the war, it wasn't until December 31, 1946, that President Truman issued a proclamation of formal cessation officially bringing hostilities of the second world war to an end. It was the costliest war in terms of casualties and expense. Over 50 countries were involved, and its effects were felt throughout the whole world. It is impossible to calculate the total cost in human life, but estimates range from 55 million to over 60 million deaths, more than in any other war in history. The casualties of war extended far beyond the battlefields. Many civilians were killed and maimed. Families were torn apart, and the psychological effects were far reaching. The impact of the events of the war, as well as the long term effects both physically and psychologically would be felt for many years to come.

The Long Road to Home

In a letter that was headed, Ie Shima Island, (A stone's throw from Tokyo), my dad wrote:

Dear "Ginny" -

What do you think of that heading on my letter? Pretty fancy, or what? (or maybe it's corny!)

I couldn't finish the letter that I started last night because the fellows [back at the tent] decided to play Monopoly and they wouldn't let me be until I played too. The first game didn't last very long so we played another one too. I was the third one to go broke in the first game and I won the second one. I'm getting pretty good in my old age.

203

Well I guess I'll answer your letter of Aug 6th now. I see both of your letters that I received yesterday were written on the same day.

Your letter here is in answer to the one I wrote about T.D. Well I would have taken that forty-five day furlough, if it was still on, because I sure would like to get back there and see you again. Now that the war is over though, I wouldn't take the T.D. They've put a new clause in the paper you sign, saying that you will return to this Command at the completion of your forty-five days at home. I wouldn't mind too much, coming back here if the war was still on, but as it is now, when I ever get home I want to stay there. The way they have this T.D. set up now, I believe it would be all right for a fellow that wanted to make a career of the Army. That would give them a chance to go home for a few days, and then come back and get overseas time in, by serving in the Army of Occupation. That's something that I don't want to do, because I'm not an Army man. I've got my own plans for the future, and I don't want the Army or anyone else telling me what to do. I want to get back there now and get myself a good job, and then settle down and get married.

I don't know how long it's going to take them to get around to sending us home now, but I sure hope that it's soon. There are a lot of rumors going around as to what's going to happen now, but of course you can't take any stock in them. There are always rumors floating around in the Army, so you get so that you don't pay any attention to them after a while. I guess all we can do is wait and see what they decided to do. I'll let you know if anything new turns up.

Ie Shima, August 20, 1945

Dear "Ginny" -

I guess it's about time I got around to writing to you again, don't you think? I haven't heard from you now for a couple of days, so I haven't got any of your letters to answer.

I sure got a surprise today. I got a letter from my mother and she told me that my sister, Virginia had a baby girl on August 10th. I almost fell over when I heard that, because she wasn't expecting it until the latter part of September. She and the baby are both coming along fine though, so I sure was glad to hear that. I was hoping that either she or Helen would get a baby girl, so now I got my wish.

I finally got a letter from Gussie yesterday and he's in the Philippines now. I thought he was over in Okinawa, but I was wrong. He's down somewhere near Manila I guess, according to his A.P.O. number. It sure was swell hearing from him again. He's with the 13th Air Force and flying a B-25. I guess he really likes that plane by the way he talks. I hope he gets sent up around here someplace so we can see each other.

Well "Ginny," I guess I'll close for this time, hoping to hear from you again real soon. Send my best regards to your mother and father.

I'll be seeing you.
All my love,
Lou

P.S. I'll probably be seeing you in a couple of months or so if things keep going the way they are now. I'll explain it to you in my next letter.

Ie Shima, August 26, 1945

We went to choir practice last night, and our Chaplain told us that he was leaving for the States this morning. I sure was surprised when he told us that. He was kind of surprised too, because his orders just came through unexpectedly yesterday morning. We hated to see him go, in one way, because he was a really swell Chaplain, but if he can get back to the States, more power to him.

By the way, in my last letter I told you that I would probably be seeing you soon, and that I'd explain it to you in this letter. Well in the first place, they've sent home every man in our group that had 85 points or more, and I have 79 points as you know, so that puts me right near the top of the list now. According to the news, they're supposed to have a re-count very soon now, and they're also going to lower the critical score to 80 or less, so I'll have more than enough points for discharge. According to that, I have high hopes of being home for Christmas. Most of the fellows here with 75 points or more have the same idea, but of course that's only our opinion, and we're not sure about it .

I've been busy these past couple of days making a model boat. It's supposed to be a battleship, the "U.S.S New Mexico," but it isn't coming out very good. It isn't quite finished yet, but it will be in a day or two. I am also making a model of a P-47 "Thunderbolt," that I started today. If it comes out any good, I'll pack it up and send it to you. It will probably take me about a week to finish it, but I'll let you know when it's done and how it looks.

Well we're starting in to be soldiers again now. Starting today we're supposed to salute all officers, have physical training every day except Sunday, and have daily inspections of our tents. We haven't done any of that now since we came overseas. Of course we've had tent inspections every once in a while, but that's about all. We're also going to have to wear our stripes and Fifth Air Force shoulder patches in a few days. That's going to seem kind of strange at first, I suppose, but at least it will get us in practice for when we get back to the States again.

I'm enclosing three pictures for you in this letter. They're not very clear, but you don't want to mind that. ...one is of Ernie Pyle's grave.

Ie Shima, September 1, 1945

Ernie Pyle was one of America's most famous and beloved news correspondents. On April 18, 1945, Ernie Pyle died on the island of Ie Shima when he was hit by Japanese machine-gun fire. He was buried on Ie Shima and eventually his body was moved to the National Memorial Cemetery of the Pacific located in Honolulu.

(From the Sven L. Sandstrom collection)
Ernie Pyle Memorial on the Island of Ie Shima

I received your letter of Aug 20th and I sure was glad to hear from you again. I'll forgive you for not writing sooner, seeing that you thought I might have been on my way home. I guess everybody back there thought that when I told them that I had applied for T.D. I don't know how long it will be before I am on my way home, but I'll let you know when that day arrives.

We heard some good news on the radio today. They've lowered the critical score to 80 now, and they're also going to give credit for time from V-E Day to V-J Day. That gives us 8 more points for overseas time, so I now have 87 points, which is more than enough for discharge. That raises my hope a little higher that I'll be home for Christmas, and I sure hope I'm right.

Our Commander called a meeting tonight to thank us all for the wonderful work that we've done in the outfit. He also said that the original bunch of fellows that came overseas with the outfit will be going home d--- soon now, and that we should train our replacements to carry on the good work that we have done. I hope he's right when he says that we'll be on our way home soon.

Ie Shima, September 3, 1945

Well they've stopped censorship regulations now, so we can write anything that we want to in our letters. We'll also be able to send home any pictures that we haven't been able to send before this. I sent home a few to my mother and father already, because I don't want to carry them around any longer. My father is making up an album of all the pictures that I've been sending home, and I guess he must have quite a few by now.

Well the P-47 that I'm making is all finished now, except for the stand for it. I worked on the stand all day today. I guess there was a little more work to it than I figured. It looks pretty good so far, so I hope I don't spoil it with the finishing touches.

The rumors are going around fast and thick now. Lately they've been saying that we're going to go to Japan first, and then go home from there, and some fellows have been saying that we're going to stay here while all of us old fellows go home, then the rest of the outfit will go to Japan. The latest one now is that all of the original men that came overseas with the outfit will be leaving here within two weeks. I hope that's true, but of course you can't take stock in them rumors. I've been inclined to think that I won't be leaving until next month, but now I hear that the re-count or the point system is effective as of Sept 2nd, so maybe I'll be home this month instead. I'm fairly certain that I'll be home for Christmas, and the way things look now, there's a chance that I'll be there for Thanksgiving. That sure would be nice and I hope that I am there by then. I'd like to be there for your birthday, but I don't know about that. Of course there's a slight chance I will be, but I believe that's only a remote possibility. I can dream though, can't I?

I'd like to have been walking along the beach with you in the moonlight. You should see some of the moonlight nights we have over here. Boy are they beautiful! The only trouble is they don't do me any good. I'll settle for a good old New England moonlight night though, and you to keep me company.

Ie Shima, September 6, 1945

(From the Sven L. Sandstrom collection)
Caption on back of picture taken on Ie Shima on Sept 5, 1945:
1st row - Ed Holmes, Murray Weiss, John Mihaila
2nd row - Bill Hennigan, Phil Marcus, and "yours truly"
in the background on the left of the picture,
you can just about see Okinawa in the distance

The way the rumors are going around here now, I'm inclined to think that I'll be on my way home in the very near future. Fifth Air Force has sent in for all of our records to see how many men are eligible to go home now, and they claim that all men with 85 or more will be going on the next quota. I've got 87, so that puts me right in there. Our Orderly Room is fixing up all of our records and everything too, so that they'll be all ready in case they send for a quota in a hurry. Maybe I'll be home for Thanksgiving, at that, and maybe for your birthday too. I sure hope anyway.

I'm enclosing four pictures for you in this letter...one is me. Here's a diagram of what the things on the sign are:

Ie Shima, September 10, 1945

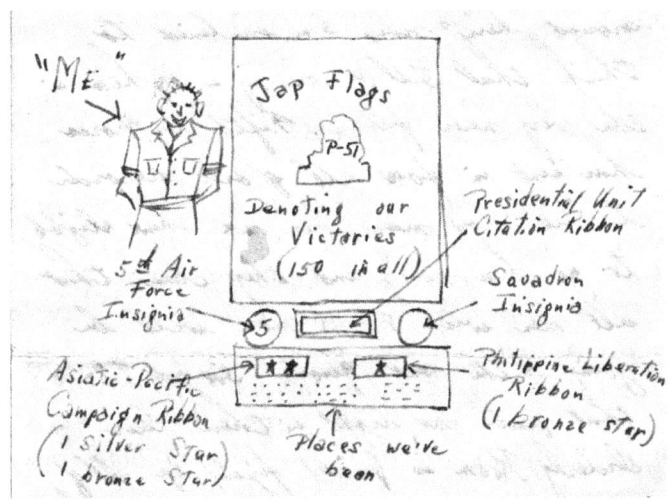

(From the Sven L. Sandstrom collection)

From all the talk that's going around here now, we'll be leaving here very soon. and I do mean <u>soon</u>. Rumor has it that we'll be leaving within a week. That's not definite, you understand, but we're all pretty certain of it. That includes all men with 80 points or more, and I have 89, so that includes me.

By the way, I have 92 points now instead of 87, because we were just authorized another battle star that we should have gotten a long time ago. It was for the Northern Solomons Campaign. We get credit for that star as far as the points are concerned, because that campaign took place before V-E Day. I don't exactly need the points because I have enough anyway, but those five extra points won't do me any harm.

They've been calling all the men with 80 points and above up to the Orderly Room the past couple of days to check over the Service Records, Medical Records and things like that, so they'll all be in order in case they call for a quota of men in a hurry. My records are all straightened out now, so they can call me any time they want to, and the sooner the better.

Ie Shima, September 12, 1945

Dear "Ginny," -

I still haven't got any of your letters to answer, but I've got to write to you anyway, because I've got some great news for you. Remember I told you that all men with 80 points and over had their Service Records, Medical Records, etc. all checked over? Well today we all had our clothing checked, and gave our forwarding addresses. That means that we're all ready to leave now in a moment's notice, in case they call for a quota of men in a hurry.

Everyone seems to think that we'll be leaving here in two or three days now, and the way they're rushing us in getting our records and everything all straightened up, I'm inclined to agree with them. I imagine our first stop will be Manila, although we may go to Okinawa instead. All we do there anyway, is to go to some Replacement depot, get our records checked again, get new clothing issued, and then leave for the States. It probably takes about one or two weeks at the most at the Replacement camp, to go through all the processing, - then we leave for Frisco.

The way things look now, I may be home for your birthday and I sure hope so. I won't say for sure that I'll be there by then, but I'll be pretty close to it anyway. It seems kind of funny to us to be saying that we're going home in a couple of days now, after being away for so long. (28 months to be exact). It sure makes a fellow feel good though, and I'm not kidding.

You may as well stop writing to me now, because by the time you get this letter, I'll be on my way to the States. I'll keep writing to you though, to keep you informed as to where I am, etc. Most likely I'll be writing a few more letters from here, because I don't expect to leave for a few days yet. I'll let you know as soon as we leave though.

Ie Shima, September 14, 1945

Dear "Ginny," -

Hi, here I am again. I'm just writing a short letter to let you know of the latest developments. There are two rumors going around now, and they both sound very good. First of all, our First Sergeant told

213

us that Group Headquarters called up and said that there is a very good possibility of some of the 85 point and over men leaving sometime tonight. They probably won't get around to taking us all tonight, but if they don't, then the rest of us will leave sometime tomorrow. The other rumor is that there is a boat out in the harbor now waiting to take us to Manila. We're supposed to get on the boat by tomorrow noon time, and then I'm fairly certain that we'll be leaving either tonight or tomorrow at the latest. I've got my barracks bag all ready now with my stuff that I'm going to take with me, and I've got the rest of my extra clothing and junk all ready to turn in to the Q.M. Supply. All they have to do now is to call me, and I'll be ready to go in a minute. It looks like I'll be there for your birthday after all. (I hope.)

Well "Ginny," please don't mind the short letter, but I want to write a few more letters before I go to bed. Send my best regards to your mother and father.

I'll be seeing you,
All my love,
Lou

Ie Shima, September 15, 1945

I'm sorry I haven't written for the past few days, but we had quite a storm here, and it disrupted everything. We've been busy the last couple of days cleaning up the mess it did to our camp area. The wind blew down quite a few of the tents around here, and mine was one of them that was blown down. The storm lasted for two days and two nights. That hurricane we had back in '38 was a picnic compared to this. Between the wind and the rain, I don't know which was worse.

We succeeded in keeping our tent up the first night, but the second night we weren't so lucky. We were out in the rains soaked to the skin, tying ropes and hammering down stakes, but the wind got the better of us, so we had to evacuate. We went up to the mess hall and spent the remainder of the night there. Everything is just about back to normal again and I hope it stays that way now, at least until we get out of here.

All we're doing now is waiting for transportation and then we'll be on our way. I don't know how long that will take, but it shouldn't be any more than a day or two at the most. I'll let you know as soon as we leave.

Ie Shima, September 20, 1945

Dear "Ginny," -

I just received your letter of September 13th, and I sure was glad to hear from you. I suppose you're surprised to see that I'm still here, but I guess we'll just have to wait until we can get some transportation. The latest rumor now is that we'll be leaving here Monday at the latest, so that's only three more days at the most. They claim that the boats and planes have been alerted to take troops to Japan, but they're through with that for a while now, so they took the ships off the alert, and they can be used for shipping men home now. I hope they're right because I'm sick of hanging around here now, and I want to go home. We have plenty to do here, in the way of sports and everything, but even at that, it's just so much time being wasted. Especially in my case anyway, because I want to get home, get a job, and settle down to normal again. I suppose a few days like this doesn't make much difference anyway, after being over here for twenty-eight months already, but still it gets tiresome just waiting around. Well, I'll let you know as soon as we leave here, and I sure hope that it's soon.

Boy, was I surprised when you said that Gus has been reported "missing." That's the first I had heard about that. This is a heck of a time to be missing. It's just as bad during war time too, but it just seems worse now to hear something like that when the war is over. I sure hope that they find him and that he's alright. I received a letter from my mother last night, and she was saying that she had just received a letter from him. That was Sept. 5th that she wrote that letter, and that's the latest letter I've received from her. I don't know whether to write to the Tangrings now or not, or wait until I get home. I'd have a heck of a job trying to think of what to write to them. It was the same way when Russell was reported missing, and I wrote to his folks and Gurlie. Maybe I'd better wait until I get home, then go up to see them, and hope that in the meantime he's found safely.

I haven't sent in anymore lessons on my refrigeration course as yet because I sent all of my books to home. I figured I'd be leaving soon so I packed up all my personal belongings and sent them home. I didn't feel like carrying all of that junk around with me. This course that I'm taking is run by the Army, but we get all of our books and everything from the International Correspondence School. Their main branch in the States is at Madison, Wisconsin, so when I get back home, I'm going to see if I can't transfer over to them so I can continue the course. I can study on it in my spare time back there, and it shouldn't take more than two or three months at the most to finish it. Who knows, it may help me some. The first thing I want to do is to go out to Norton's and get in there again if it's possible, then I can be working and studying at the same time. When I finish the course, I can look around and get some information about it then start to work in some plant and get some more experience. Then maybe I can work myself up and amount to something someday. I can always go to the Veterans Administration and they can give me all the information I want, and they will even try to place me someplace where I can get started. I don't know how all of this is going to work out, but there's nothing like trying.

Gee, I'm sorry to hear that you've been having trouble with your appendix. I hope you're not in the hospital when I get home. In fact, you'd better not be. After all, we won't be able to go out if you're up there. I expect to be home around the first part of November, as far as I know right now, so you'll have to wait with your operation until after your birthday anyway. I hope you won't have to go at all, but I suppose you've got to if the doctor says so.

Ie Shima, September 21, 1945

Hello again. How is every little thing with you these days? Good, I hope. I'm feeling just fine, but I'm getting sick and tired of just hanging around here and waiting. I just got through playing a couple of games of Monopoly. At least it's something to do to pass the time away anyway. It gets kind of monotonous just sitting down and writing letters or reading all day long.

Well "Ginny," it looks as though we'll finally be on our way tomorrow. They just told us today that all men with 80 points and over are going to be transferred over to a Bomb Group here on the island for transportation. We're supposed to leave tomorrow morning. They're transferring all men in all the Air Force outfits here with 80 points and more into the Bomb Group, and the Bomb Group is transferring all their men with 79 points and under, to all the outfits here. All in all, it's just an exchange of men. Well anyway, when all this transferring back and forth is all done, then the Bomb Group is going to go back to the States as a unit. They claim that we'll be leaving for the States on the 27th or 29th, so if we do, then there's a good chance that I'll be home for your birthday. I'll probably be able to find out more about it when I get over there, and if I can, I'll write and let you know about it. I hope we don't get any more hurricanes or anything now to prevent us from leaving this time.

Well "Ginny," I guess I'll close for this time, but I'll write again as soon as I can find out any more news as to how long it will take us to get home, or anything like that.

Ie Shima, September 23, 1945

We finally moved out of the 342nd, and we are now in the 43rd Bomb Group. We moved over here yesterday, and it's only about a mile or so from our old camp area. We're still using our old address though, because we bring our mail over there every day to be sent out, instead of sending it from here. I was going to write to you yesterday, but we were busy all day getting set up and everything, and at night we didn't have any lights set up in the tent, so we just went to bed instead. I haven't the slightest idea as to how long we'll be here before they ship us home, but I don't think it will be too long. There are a lot of rumors going around as usual, but of course you can't take any stock in them. Everyone seems to think that we'll be out of here about the first of the month, and I'm inclined to agree with them. Even if we stay here for two weeks, which I doubt very much, we should still be home around the first part of November. I'm keeping my fingers crossed, and I'll let you know if anything new comes up.

Ie Shima, September 25, 1945

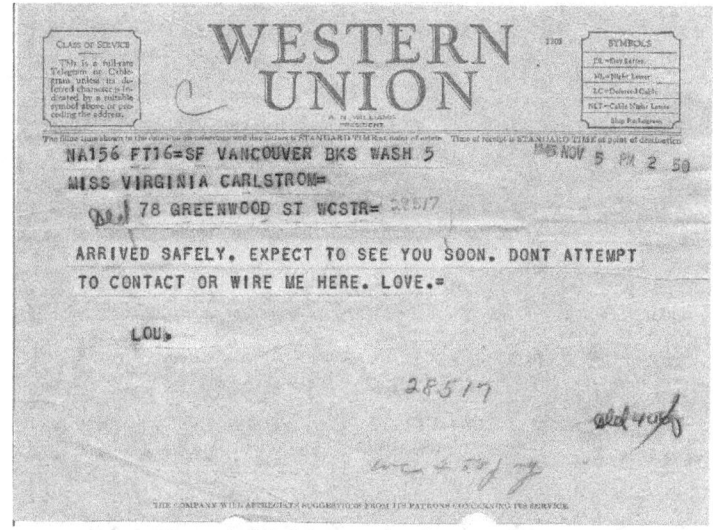

(From the H. Virginia Sandstrom collection)
Western Union Telegram, dated November 5, 1945,
sent by my dad to my mom when he arrived in the States.
"Arrived safely. Expect to see you soon.
Don't attempt to contact me here. Love, Lou."

Dear "Ginny," -

Well I'm finally getting around to writing to you again. It's been quite a while now since I've done any writing, but I hope you'll forgive me. - Thank you, Dear, I knew you would.

219

How is every little thing with you these days? Good, I hope. I'm feeling just fine and glad to be back in the good old U.S.A. again. We arrived in Portland, Oregon the other day, and came up here to Vancouver Barracks. I sent you a telegram yesterday, and also a birthday card, so I hope you got them all right. I thought for sure that I was going to be home today for your birthday, but we were delayed for a while on Okinawa on account of the Typhoon, which you probably read about in the papers. I'll tell you all about that when I see you again. Well anyway, we'll have to celebrate your birthday when I get home, which will be very soon now.

We're leaving for Fort Devens at nine o'clock tonight, so we should be there in about four or five days. I'm going to call up as soon as I get there, and I'll let you know approximately when I'll be home. They have to check over our records again when we get there, and issue us some more clothes and stuff, so that will take a few days. Sometimes they give the fellows thirty day furloughs a couple of days after they get there, and then they have to go back and get their discharge papers, or they make you wait about a week or so and give you the discharge papers right away. I'll probably find out what they're going to do with us when we get there, and then I'll let you know when I call up. At least I'll be home before Thanksgiving anyway, no matter how they do it.

I've got an awful lot to tell you and everything, but I guess I'll have to wait until I see you again. I'm in a hurry now, because I have to eat supper, then we've got to report for roll call and get our baggage together and get ready to leave. I hope your appendix hasn't been bothering you too much, and I'm keeping my fingers crossed that you won't be in

220

the hospital when I get home. Well "Ginny," please don't mind the short letter, but I've got to rush over and eat now and get ready. Send my best regards to your mother and father.

**I'll be seeing you
All my Love,
Lou**

Vancouver, Washington, November 6, 1945

(From the H. Virginia Sandstrom collection)

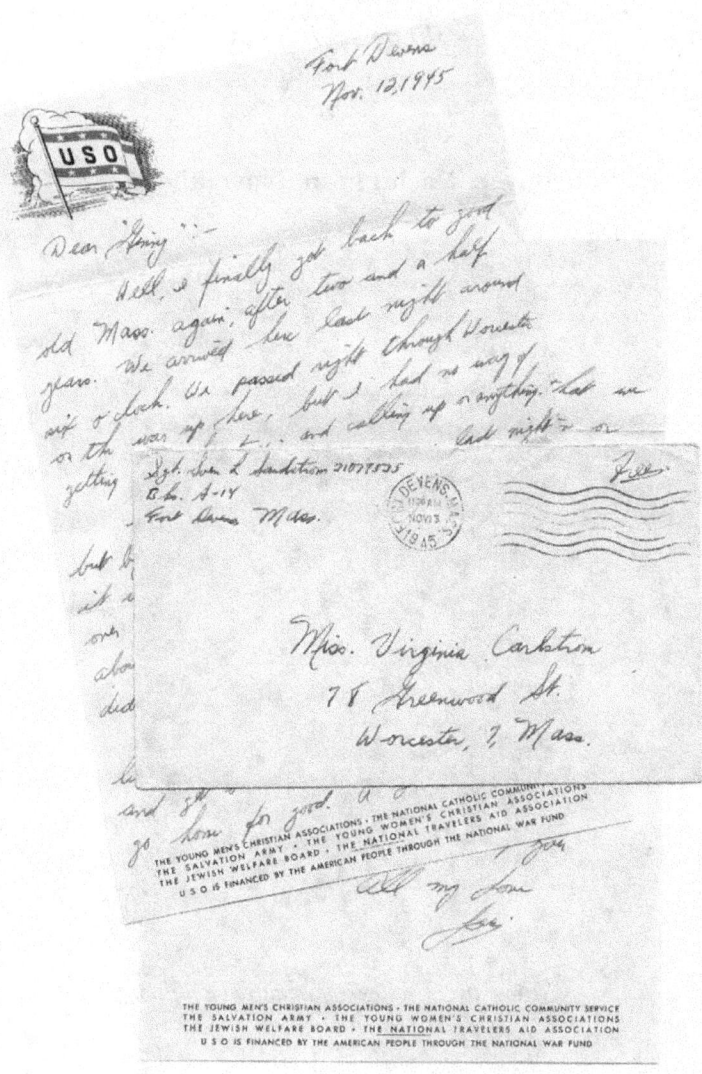

(From the H. Virginia Sandstrom collection)
The last letter before returning home.

Dear "Ginny" -

Well, I finally got back to good old Massachusetts again, after two and a half years. We arrived here last night around six o-clock. We passed right through Worcester on the way up here, but I had no way of getting off the train and calling up or anything.

I was going to call you last night but by the time they got through with us it was around 9:30 P.M., and then I went over to the telephone building and there were about fifty fellows waiting for calls, so I didn't bother with it.

Well, we don't get any furloughs here like I thought we would. We wait here and get our discharge , and then we go home for good. A Lt. was speaking to us today, and he told us that we should be out of here in about two or three days at the most. In that case, I should be home around Wednesday, Thursday., or Friday sometime. Most likely it will be Thursday. We'll find out for sure tomorrow or the next day, and then I'll try to call you up and let you know, so you'll know when to expect me.

Well "Ginny," I'll close for now, but I'll be seeing you in a few days. Give my best regards to your mother and father.

I'll be seeing you
All my Love

Lou

Fort Devens, Massachusetts, November 12, 1945

On Wednesday, November 14, 1945, my dad received his formal honorable discharge from the United States Army Air Corps. He earned the Good Conduct Medal, Victory Medal, Asiatic Pacific Theater Campaign Ribbon, Distinguished Unit Badge, and the Philippines Liberation Ribbon with two Bronze Service Stars.

After three and a half years in military service, two and a half years serving overseas, my dad's deepest desire came to be true. He finally returned to his home in "good old Worcester, Massachusetts."

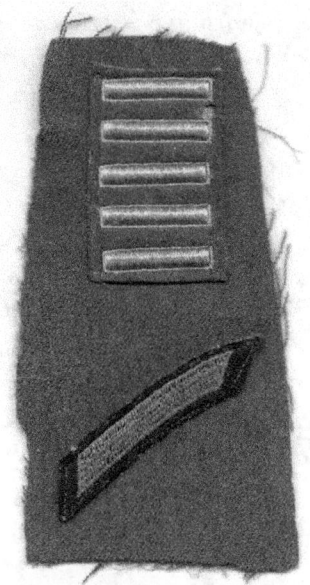

(From the Sven L. Sandstrom collection)
Service stripes from my dad's uniform.
Each of the five service stripes represents six months of overseas service.
The larger stripe represents honorable overseas service.
My dad served overseas from June 1943 - October 1945.

Afterword

I do not have the details of my father's homecoming; however, it must have been a mix of joy and sadness. It was a different world than what he had left behind three and a half years previously. For one thing, some of my dad's childhood friends were killed or had been changed by the war. The pain of loss was reflected in the family and friends of those killed in action.

Perhaps the most heart-breaking news for my dad upon his return home, was when he learned that one of his best buddies was killed on August 16, 1945. 2nd Lt. Gustaf "Gus" Tangring, was co-pilot of a five man crew on a B-25, assigned to the 13th Air Force, 42nd Bombardment Group, 70th Bombardment Squadron. The plane disappeared somewhere in the Southwest Pacific along the flight route between Biak and Morotai. The crew was declared dead that same day.

(Photographed by Marie Sturdevant)
The memorial plaque for 2nd Lt. "Gus" Tangring at Tangring Square,
(Greenwood St and Wiser Ave, Worcester, Massachusetts)

I remember my mom telling me that my dad had changed when he came home after the war. He had problems with anxiety, including sleep disorder and difficulties with being in crowded places. In present day, the display of these symptoms following a traumatic event is commonly referred to as post traumatic stress disorder. This was a common problem for the returning G.I.'s. There was no recognition of this syndrome at that time, let alone any planned treatment for those returning from the war. Many turned the horrors of war inward and never talked about what they had seen. As for my dad, these attacks came less frequently over time and he was able to return to a normal life. However, there was something buried deep inside that must have haunted him for the rest of his life. There was so much he never shared, and a part of his life remained a mystery.

(From the H. Virginia Sandstrom collection)

Even though the world had seen so much death and destruction through the war years, a new hope of a better world was rising up from the ashes of devastation from the war. The end of the war was followed by economic expansion known as the post war economic boom and the Golden Age of Capitalism. Political relations between the former Axis powers and Western Allies were quickly normalized as both sides did not want to experience another economic downturn as seen post World War I.

Perhaps one of the biggest contributing factors in the economic growth following World War II was the introduction of *The Servicemen's Readjustment Act of 1944,* also known as the G.I. Bill. The purpose of this bill was to help returning G.I.'s through the process of re-integration into civilian life. These were the same individuals who had grown up in a world of economic instability and lack of job security in the years leading up to the war. Now they were returning to a world where higher education and home ownership were encouraged through the benefits provided by the G.I. Bill. These benefits were available to all veterans who had served in active duty during the war years, for at least ninety days, and had received an honorable discharge. Combat duty was not a requirement. Among the benefits were low interest mortgages, low interest loans to start farms and businesses, and tuition to attend college or vocational school. This resulted in an increase in home ownership with many families moving to suburban developments. With more people achieving higher education leading to a more skilled work force, the average family incomes increased making it more possible to achieve the American dream. The post war years saw an increase in the number of births which is commonly referred to as the Baby Boom. Life was easier and jobs were more plentiful.

(From the H. Virginia Sandstrom collection)

(From the H. Virginia Sandstrom collection)
My parent's wedding picture, November 29,1947

(From the H. Virginia Sandstrom collection)
My parent's wedding picture, November 29,1947.
Standing up for them were their friends, Russell and Gurlie Anderson

Two years after his homecoming, on November 29, 1947, my dad and mom were married. They made their home in Worcester, Massachusetts. He worked in the office at Bayer and Mingolla Construction Company in Millbury, Massachusetts. On July 23, 1953, their first son, Paul Louis was born. Three years later, on November 9, 1956, I was born.

(From the H. Virginia Sandstrom collection)
Mom and Dad with Paul, December 1955.

(From the H. Virginia Sandstrom collection)
My dad and I in the spring of 1957.

On June 17, 1967, Paul died in a drowning accident at the age of thirteen. I was ten at the time. The next day, Sunday June 18th, visiting hours were held at Lindquist Funeral Home in Worcester. It was Father's Day. I have a vivid memory of my dad at the moment he saw Paul for the first time in the casket. His broken heart could endure no more as he crumbled on the kneeling bench beside the casket and sobbed. There was no greater sorrow that either of my parents had ever experienced.

On Friday December 11, 1987, I received a call that my dad was taken by ambulance to the hospital. Four days later, on December 15th, my dad passed away from heart failure, and pneumonia. He was buried at the New Swedish Cemetery in Worcester, alongside Paul.

After my mom passed away on February 9, 2007, I began searching through boxes of pictures and letters. I found an album of pictures from the war along with a collection of over 200 letters and several V-mails from my dad to my mom. Finding the letters that my dad sent to her during the war was a gift. As I read through them I learned so much about who he was and what his experiences were like as he served overseas in the Pacific war. The more I read, the more I wanted to understand, and the more I wanted to share his story.

So many children of the World War II generation have questions about the lives of their parents and their parents' contemporaries. This was a generation who grew up with very little in terms of material possessions, but were grounded more in the basic values of life: faith, family and friends. They didn't have much; didn't expect much; and in their youthful splendor, they sacrificed so much, and in many instances, even their own lives. These are our parents and grandparents. There is a certain beauty and wisdom in the sunset of their lives. The opportunities to hear their stories will soon be lost. Listen while you can...cherish those times...listen, and listen again. I am now convinced, more than ever, they were more than ordinary people. They were in fact extraordinary people who lived through extraordinary times.

SVEN L SANDSTROM
SGT US ARMY AIR FORCES
WORLD WAR II
MAR 13 1921   DEC 15 1987

ABOUT THE AUTHOR

When I was a child, I liked to write short stories and I dreamed of writing a book. My mom wisely told me to write about something that I knew from my own life. Writing was in me, but so was science. Even though the career path I chose was in clinical laboratory science, I still had a desire to write, even taking an evening course in Short Story Writing. The demands of work and time spent raising a family left me with little opportunity to pursue writing; so I tucked that dream away for sometime in the future.

As my children were growing and becoming more independent, I decided to answer an ad, writing local stories for the town newspaper. Working as a news correspondent, writing human interest stories for the local paper was a good experience, but short-lived due to my job at the hospital and caring for my aging mother. Even though she was experiencing failing health, she organized family pictures, documents and genealogy charts.

When my mom passed away in 2007, I continued with her genealogy work. Among the papers and pictures I found were the letters my dad wrote to during WWII. Over the next four years I documented my findings into a private book to be shared with my family. When that project was completed, I began reading through my father's letters and looking through his pictures from overseas. I began to see a story taking shape; one that was meant to be discovered and shared, I believed, through me.

As I began taking excerpts from the letters and putting them into a word document, the story of my father's wartime experiences began to take on a life of its own. This is where I saw my childhood dream beginning to become a reality. Not only was I writing the book dreamed about so long ago, but I was sharing in this journey with my parents, years after they passed from this life.

There was so much about my father that I did not understand and his passing had left me with many unresolved feelings. Researching and documenting the events in this book became my journey towards understanding, healing and self-discovery. There has been a longing within me to know more about who my father was. Through the process of writing this book, I have been able to connect with my father and to honor his life.

Another amazing and unexpected gift received along this journey was the connection I made with René Palmer Armstrong, author of the book *Wings and a Ring*. As I was looking through a magazine rack at a local bookstore, I came across the magazine, *America in WWII*, where I found an ad for her book. I ordered the book through her website and made the personal contact with René. Through her guidance and encouragement, I was able to work through the process of creating this book. Since that chance encounter, she has become my mentor and very special friend.

This book is a gift for my children, Christine and Robert, that they may understand and learn more about the grandfather whom they never had the chance to know. It is my sincere desire that this book will inspire others to learn more about the Greatest Generation and give thanks for the sacrifices they made in order to secure the freedoms that we enjoy today.

Marie L. Sturdevant

Recommended reading

Image courtesy of René Palmer Armstrong

Wings and a Ring: Letters of War and Love from a WWII Pilot
by René Palmer Armstrong

This book captures the human side of war through the lives and experiences of World War II pilot, James Richard Jones, and his fiancée, Helen Elnora Bartlett. Their journey is documented in the letters from J.R. to his sweetheart, Elnora, while he was stationed in the jungles of New Guinea. The story is enriched with details from historical records, and official declassified government documents and military records.

In this profound and insightful story, the reader will gain a sense of the daily struggles of a pilot while dealing with the hardships of separation and the hope of the enduring promises of love.

www.wingsandaring.com